Living A Life That Really Matters

Michael Snyder

-CONTENTS-

-CHAPTER ONE-

"God Can Take The Broken Pieces Of Your Life And Turn Them Into A Beautiful Thing."

About 20 years ago, my life was a total mess. My career was going absolutely nowhere, I was deeply depressed because the woman that I had loved had married someone else, most of my friends had abandoned me, my health was in very bad shape, and I was generally a pretty miserable person to be around. Literally next to nobody knew who I was, and even fewer people cared if I lived or if I died. At that moment it would have been really difficult for anyone to imagine that I had much of anything to look forward to, and my prospects seemed to be dimming with each passing day.

So if you have ever hit rock bottom in your life, I can identify with you.

But no matter how bad things ever got, I never gave up. I eventually pulled myself together and went to law school, and after law school I worked as an attorney in the heart of Washington D.C. for a number of years.

While working in D.C., I met and married an absolutely spectacular woman, and now we have been married for over a decade and we have a wonderful two-year-old daughter. She is a bundle of energy, and I am very thankful that my wife is nine years younger than I am because she has the energy to keep up with her.

It was also during our time in D.C. that I discovered something called blogging. At the time that I started, there were already more than a million other blogs out there, and so I wondered why anyone would ever want to read what I had to share. And when I started with a few small blogs my readership was so tiny that you could have measured it with a microscope, but I kept going.

And that is one of the keys in life. Often those that end up being "successful" are those that simply refuse to quit.

Anyone can start something, but not everyone has the passion to keep on going when things get really tough.

Eventually my readership began to build, and in late 2009 I started The Economic Collapse Blog. Since that time, my websites have been viewed well over 100 million times, and my articles are regularly republished on many of the largest and most popular alternative news websites in the entire world.

In addition to my websites, I am touching the world through my books, and I am a regular guest on radio and television shows all over the nation. Nearly six years ago my wife and I moved out to the mountains of Idaho, and it always amazes us how we can impact lives literally all over the planet from our quiet home in the hills.

Over the course of this crazy journey that my wife and I have been on I have certainly learned a lot of very important lessons. Like most of us, from a very early age there was something deep inside of me that yearned to live a life that really matters, but there were times when it looked like there was no possible way that was ever going to happen. During those dark times, I felt like my life was destined to be rather meaningless, and I felt powerless to do anything about it. But of course with God all things are possible. If you are deeply hurting right now, I want you to know that God can take the broken pieces of your life and turn them into a beautiful thing. This is something that I am going to tell you all throughout this book, and by the final chapter I hope that many of you will start to believe it.

In this book I am going to share with you some of my most important secrets. If I had not discovered these secrets, I would definitely not be the person that I am today. Some of these secrets will be easy to grasp intellectually, but putting them into practice on a daily basis is where the challenge will be. It is the things that we do consistently that determine who we really are, and if you start doing the things that I am about to share with you on a consistent basis your life will be completely transformed for the better.

Each of us only gets one chance at life. So why waste it? It is so easy to get caught up in all of the things that we feel we are supposed to do, and many people spend their entire lives trying to meet the expectations of others.

My hope is that this book will help a lot of people out there start to come alive again. When we were kids, all of us were full of life, but somewhere along the way most of us end up losing that spark. Life is meant to be lived with passion, and you don't have to lose that passion as you age. In fact, I believe that the final chapters of your life can be the best chapters of all.

No matter how bad things may seem right now, God is not done with you yet. There is always a way to turn things around, and even if it seems impossible right now, God can make a way where there seems to be no way.

This book is unlike anything that I have ever done before. Most of my other writing is about the key economic, political, social and spiritual issues of our day, but this book addresses matters of the heart that everybody deals with on a daily basis. In our society today, so many live in defeat, and my hope is that what I have to share will help large numbers of people to break the chains that are holding them back and start living free again.

You don't have to be rich or famous to live a life that really matters. In fact, a lot of those that are rich and famous are absolutely squandering the opportunities that they have been given to do great things with their lives.

And I do not intend to teach you how to be rich or how to be famous. If you want one of those books, there are literally thousands of them out there. What I want to do in this book is to help you start to become the person that God created you to be. God's plan for your life is far better than your plan, and when we surrender to Him it opens up all sorts of possibilities.

Living a life that really matters means that you have a purpose that is far greater than just trying to satisfy your own selfish wants and desires. It means that you have a reason to get up in the morning and a destiny to fulfill. And it means that you are willing to fight for the people and the causes that you love.

Many of the truths in this book may sound simple, but if you actually go ahead and diligently apply them they will transform your life in ways that you may not even be able to imagine right now. Every life is meant to be a light, and if we allow the love of God to shine through us we can literally light up the entire planet.

Yes, incredible challenges are ahead for both the United States and the world as a whole. I have certainly not changed my perspective on that at all. But the principles in this book will help you to live a life of meaning and purpose no matter how crazy events around us become.

God did not create you to live a mediocre life. He created you to live an overflowing life, and no matter how messed up things are right now you can still have that.

And ultimately we are meant to live in overflow as a community. When we work together we are greater than the sum of our parts, and if we are willing to have just a little bit of faith we can dramatically change the course of history.

God is raising up a Remnant all over the world, and this Remnant is going to turn this world completely upside down for Jesus Christ. No matter what challenges may confront us, we will not bend, we will not bow, and we will not break. Even against seemingly insurmountable odds we will take our stand, and history will remember us as a generation that had faith to believe the impossible, that had hope when it seemed like all hope was lost, and that loved one another and our King with an undying love that could not be shaken.

In this book you may find that I repeat certain concepts in several different ways. There is a reason for this. Studies have shown that one of the keys to human learning is repetition. For example, my little daughter had to see the letters of the alphabet many, many times before she started to recognize any of them. As adults, we are very much the same way, and I am going to try to hammer home the most important points in this book using multiple approaches.

And this book is not for speed readers. In some ways this book is modeled after the Book of Proverbs, and those of you that have read the Book of Proverbs already know that it takes time to digest. I have embedded little "truth bombs" into every chapter, and if you come across a sentence or a phrase that really speaks to you, I would encourage you to take your time to reflect on what God is ministering to your heart before moving on.

This is the most important book that I have ever written, and I am so glad that it got into your hands. I wish that someone had clearly explained these principles to me at a very early age, and it is a real privilege for me to be able to share them with you. Hopefully you will find these secrets as valuable as I have.

-CHAPTER TWO-

"If You Want To Live A Great Life, Live A Life Of Great Love."

If you want to live a great life, it isn't that complicated.

All you have to do is to start applying some very simple principles.

Actually, none of the principles that you will find in this book are mine. In fact, they have been around for a very, very long time. But if you will learn and apply these principles, they will absolutely revolutionize your life.

I know that this is true, because they are revolutionizing my life.

Let's start with something really basic. If you are like most people, virtually all of your greatest memories have something in common. Just think about this for a moment. Think back to the most wonderful highlights of your life, and see if you can figure out what is true about almost every single one of them.

Have you figured it out yet?

One thing that virtually all great memories have in common is that someone else was there. Our lives are defined by our relationships with others, and we were created to love and to be loved. Just try to think of a wonderful moment in your life that didn't involve anyone else at all. For most people, it would be quite difficult to come up with a single one. Even if one of your great memories involves being completely alone and enjoying some peace and quiet, the reason why that peace and quiet was so meaningful is because of the lack of peace and quiet in your regular daily life when you are surrounded by others.

The same thing could be said about most of your bad memories as well. Even if it is something like an illness or an injury, those experiences are given context by the people in your life. And of course the greatest sources of pain can often be those that are the closest to us.

Despite our enormous wealth and despite all of our extremely advanced technology, we have never even come close to mastering the art of human relationships. In our society today, it seems like almost everyone is unhappy. In fact, I would go as far as to say that the vast majority of the people that I have ever encountered in my life are miserable at least to some degree. Of course I have also met people that live lives filled with joy and peace, and it turns out that most of them are practicing at least some of the principles that I am going to lay out in this book.

One of the reasons why I am writing this book is to be a helping hand to those that are living lives filled with misery. My hope is that many that read this book will see that life does not have to be filled with unhappiness and despair.

Perhaps you think that I am overstating things. Unfortunately, that is not the case at all. According to the American Medical Association's Journal of Internal Medicine, one out of every six Americans is on an antidepressant or some other kind of psychiatric drug. And for certain demographic groups the rate is far higher. If you can believe it, one out of every four women in the United States in their 40s and 50s is currently on an antidepressant medication.

Overall, medical professionals in the United States write more than 250 million prescriptions for antidepressants every single year.

If we are truly "happy" as a society, then why has there been such an explosion in the demand for these types of drugs?

Others try to drown out their misery in other ways. It has been estimated that 60 million people in the United States abuse alcohol, and another 22 million Americans abuse illegal drugs.

Of course millions of others are addicted to other vices such as gambling, pornography and other forms of "entertainment".

Most people spend an enormous amount of time and energy trying to do something about the gnawing feeling of pain and emptiness that they feel deep inside. They know that they could be happy, but they have no idea how to actually get there.

One of the big reasons why there is such immense unhappiness in our society today is because people are very, very lonely. If you go back 100 years, the average U.S. household consisted of about 4.5 people, but today that figure has dropped all the way down to about 2.5 people. And we actually have a higher percentage of one person households than anyone else on the planet.

A big reason why our households are so small is because the traditional family structure is crumbling.

The only two nations that have a higher divorce rate than the United States are Belarus and the Maldives, and our families are falling apart all around us. Today, more than 40 percent of all babies are born to unmarried women, and about a third of all children are being raised in homes without a father.

What in the world has happened to us?

Over the decades, we have forgotten the importance of marriage and family, and now we have a giant mess on our hands.

According to the Pew Research Center, 72 percent of all U.S. adults were married back in 1960, but today only 51 percent of all adults are married.

And of course most people that are married in this country are not exactly happily married. In fact, some of the loneliest and unhappiest people in the entire world are currently married.

In a desperate attempt to find true happiness, most people end up chasing the things that the world says will make them happy. Of course one of the big things is money. So many people out there are convinced that if they can just make enough money that they will finally find fulfillment in life.

When I was growing up, I fell for this lie too. In high school I told my family that I was going to go into business someday and make a ton of money. Then I was going to buy a huge house that I would surround with a very tall fence and a giant moat to keep them out.

But does money actually bring happiness?

Of course not.

In my life I have had times when I have had enough money, and I have had times when I have not had enough money, and having enough money is definitely better. When you don't have enough money it can add a tremendous amount of stress to your life, but having money can bring on other sorts of problems.

Ultimately, we can learn a lot by looking at the wealthiest men and women in the world, because many of them are also among the most miserable. No amount of money could ever possibly buy you lasting fulfillment and happiness, but many people never learn this lesson and spend their entire lives chasing more wealth.

Others believe that the key to life is to be constantly learning, growing and achieving goals. And those are certainly good things, but constantly setting new hoops in front of ourselves to jump through is not the answer either. We can certainly keep ourselves distracted for a while, but the pain that is deep inside will inevitably keep returning.

One of the big trends among Millennials is to chase "experiences". Rather than trying to get a big paycheck, a big house and a big car, many of them are attempting to squeeze as much of the "juice" out of life as they possibly can. So they run around trying to "experience" everything that they possibly can, but many of them are coming to the realization that chasing "experiences" is not the secret to life either.

I could go on and on with other examples of the things that people are chasing in a desperate attempt to find fulfillment, but I think that you probably get the point by now.

Life isn't about how much you know or about how much money you have or about how good looking you are.

Rather, life is about how much you love and about how much others love you in return.

In Matthew 22:36-40, Jesus was asked a very interesting question, and his answer points us to what really matters in life...

36 Master, which is the great commandment in the law?

37 Jesus said unto him, Thou shalt love the Lord thy God with all thy heart, and with all thy soul, and with all thy mind.

38 This is the first and great commandment.

39 And the second is like unto it, Thou shalt love thy neighbour as thyself.

40 On these two commandments hang all the law and the prophets.

In the end, life is all about loving God and loving others. Of course most people don't understand how to go about doing either of those two things, and so in this book we are going to spend a good amount of time unpacking what it means to love God and what it means to love others. All of the principles in this book work together, and if you leave one of the key components out you may find that nothing that I am talking about seems to be working for you. So it is imperative to read all the way through the end of the book to see how everything works together.

Let me address one thing right away. In the verses from the book of Matthew that I quoted above, Jesus mentions "commandments", and many Americans instinctively recoil when they see that word because most of us generally do not like anyone telling us what to do.

But God is not giving us commandments just because He is trying to be bossy. Someone that I highly respect has described God's commandments as "guardrails". They keep us on the road and they let us know when we are getting off track.

Of course God never forces us to do anything. If we are really determined to drive off the road, He will allow us to do that. But He doesn't want us to drive off the road. He wants us to live great lives, and He has given us His instructions so that we will know how to do that.

In the Scriptures, we are told that there is "life" and "blessing" in keeping God's commandments, and that those that choose to reject God's instructions should expect the opposite. In my life I have been on both sides of that equation, and I can tell you that being on the side of "life" and "blessing" is much better by far.

11

And one of my favorite verses in the entire Bible is Matthew 5:19...

Whosoever therefore shall break one of these least commandments, and shall teach men so, he shall be called the least in the kingdom of heaven: but whosoever shall do and teach them, the same shall be called great in the kingdom of heaven.

I am likely to come back to that verse several more times in this book, because to me it is one of the most critical verses in the entire New Testament. And keeping His commandments begins with loving God and with loving others.

When we love, we are doing what we were designed to do. We were always meant to have deep, meaningful relationships with God and with others, but as a society we have gotten so far away from these core principles. My hope is that this book will be a positive step back in the right direction for many that will read it.

We need to realize that life is not all about pleasing ourselves. When we take our eyes off of ourselves and start truly caring about others, everything completely changes. And if we could just get everyone to start loving one another, our entire society could literally change overnight.

And the ironic thing is that self-obsessed individuals that are completely focused on making themselves happy are often the most miserable people that you would ever want to be around. True happiness is found in giving and caring and serving others, and this simple truth alone can completely change your life.

But even though almost everyone understands that they should love others, there are reasons why most people are failing miserably. In this book I am going to go back to the basics, and I am going to try to break things down in a way that everyone can understand.

And as I write this book, I am in the process of learning as well. By the end of this book, my hope is that we will have all grown tremendously.

My wife and I are always praying that God would make us into people of great love, and as I have discussed above, that is truly the key to living a great life.

So stay with me, because I truly believe that this book could end up changing your life more than just about any other book that you have ever purchased.

-CHAPTER THREE-

"Love Is Not A Feeling. Rather, Love Is A Conscious Choice That We Must Make Every Single Day."

In our culture, the word "love" has become synonymous with romantic love, and it is most often described as a feeling. My wife and I like to watch Hallmark romantic comedies, and so often in those films the lead female character is wrestling with her feelings of love for two competing suitors. Of course by the end of the movie her feelings for one of the men become overwhelming, and she ultimately chooses him.

But love is not a feeling, and it is imperative that we get people to understand this. Because no matter how strong your feelings are for a particular person, there will be times when they will inevitably fade. Some people bounce from romantic relationship to romantic relationship for years because they do not understand this basic fact.

Or let me give you another example that virtually everyone should be able to identify with. When you were younger, did you ever develop "crushes" on members of the opposite sex? When you are young and "in love", it can seem like being with that other person is a matter of life or death, but all "crushes" eventually fade and years later you may look back and wonder what you were thinking for ever being attracted to that other person in the first place.

In the previous chapter I told you that we would be going back to the basics, and one of the first things that we need to do is to establish what love is and what it is not.

Love is a choice. Some days I may have tremendous feelings of love for my family, but on other days I might be feeling extremely exhausted and those feelings may be hard to find at all. But just because my emotions may be going haywire on a particular day does not mean that I do not love my family.

In the Scriptures, more than anything else we are commanded to love, and God would not command us to do something that we are not capable of doing.

God created us to love and to be loved, but we get to make a choice as to whether we are going to live that way or not.

There is certainly nothing wrong with loving feelings. In fact, I very much encourage everyone to cultivate them as much as possible. We were created with emotions, and we should seek to nurture the ones that are positive and constructive.

And one of my pet peeves is to go to a "worship service" where everyone is just kind of sitting there going through the motions and nobody is really showing any emotion. The Bible tells us that we are to love the Lord with all of our heart, all of our soul, all of our mind and all of our strength, and somewhere along the line that is going to involve some emotion.

Some churches get criticized for being too emotional when they worship God, but in my opinion all of us need to become much more emotional about the one that created us all.

If it is okay for people to get wild and crazy over a football game, then it is certainly okay for believers to get wild and crazy for a God that loved us enough to send His Son to die on the cross for all of humanity.

But sometimes it is the people that are sitting quietly in their seats that are being the most worshipful of all. So just because we may be making the most noise does not mean that we are showing the most love. We are going to talk much more about loving God in subsequent chapters.

For the moment, I am just trying to establish that love is a choice and not a feeling. We should certainly expect that loving feelings will be the natural result of a decision to love, but so many people completely switch the order. They wait for feelings of love, and then once those feelings arrive they make a decision to love.

And we need to start thinking of love in much broader terms. So many single people out there think that they do not have "love" in their lives because they are not currently in a romantic relationship. But that is not true at all. Every relationship in our lives should be based on love, and that includes our family, our friends, our neighbors, our co-workers, and everyone else that we encounter on a regular basis.

I personally know some single people out there that live lives that are absolutely immersed in love because they are constantly seeking to cultivate very deep relationships with others. When we start understanding that non-romantic relationships can be just as deep or even deeper than romantic relationships, a whole new world begins to open up.

Not that I am denigrating romantic relationships in any way. My wife is my best friend, and we have a great marriage. And one of the keys to our marriage is that we choose to love and forgive one another every single day. I am going to talk much more about marriage in a future chapter.

Once you understand that love is a choice, then you can begin to realize that means that you can literally love anyone. Instead of "following your feelings", you can love even the most horrible and wretched people in your life because your decisions are not dictated by how you feel about them.

And love almost always involves taking action of some kind. 1 Corinthians 13 is known as "the love chapter" in the Bible, and the following is how verses four through seven are translated in the Modern English Version...

4 Love suffers long and is kind; love envies not; love flaunts not itself and is not puffed up, 5 does not behave itself improperly, seeks not its own, is not easily provoked, thinks no evil; 6 rejoices not in iniquity, but rejoices in the truth; 7 bears all things, believes all things, hopes all things, and endures all things.

There is nothing in there about waiting to "feel" a certain way. Instead, the Apostle Paul uses all sorts of action words in this passage. That is because love is far more about what we do than it is about how we feel.

If you "follow your feelings", you will find that you often discard people in your life once you have seemingly lost the "loving feelings" that you once had for them. And if you do this often enough, you may find that you end up completely and utterly alone.

Once again, I am not knocking emotion. I believe that we are to live our lives with passion, and I can't imagine that it would be possible to live a life of passion without emotion. I love emotion and I often use it to help fuel my writing and my ministry. But I do not allow my emotions to control me, nor do I allow them to make my decisions for me.

Our emotions should serve us rather than the other way around.

It is inevitable that our emotions will go up and down, and they can be highly manipulated. If we allow our emotions to rule us, we will invariably make huge mistakes that we will later regret bitterly.

The Bible instructs us to love our enemies. If we allow our emotions to make all of our decisions, that is going to be extremely difficult for us to do. But if we grasp the fact that love is a choice of the will, then suddenly that very difficult commandment becomes very possible.

Feelings come and feelings go, but love doesn't have to be that way.

True love is a conscious decision that is followed up by consistent action.

If you are a parent, this should be very easy for you to understand. You may come home some evening only to find that your young child has smeared poop all over the walls, and you may struggle with your emotions in that moment, but that does not mean that you do not love your little one. You feed your child, you clothe your child, you educate your child and you watch your child like a hawk because you deeply love your child. That is the kind of consistent action that I am talking about.

Of course not all relationships have the same intensity. I have friendships all over the country, and I may only interact with some of those friends very rarely, but I still love them.

It is not necessarily how much time you have with someone that matters, but rather what you do with that time.

One of my pet peeves is when people speak of "killing time". Time is one of the most precious resources that we have, and we should all endeavor to squeeze as much living into the limited amount of time that we have been given as we possibly can.

If you never come to the understanding that love is a decision and not a feeling, you will always be waiting to feel certain things before you give yourself permission to love. But you don't actually have to feel anything in order to love someone. Just make a decision in faith that you are going to love that person, and then follow up that decision with actions that show your love. In the next chapter we are going to discuss how to go about doing that.

It is easy to love those that are good to us, but loving those that seem very unlovable can prove to be quite a challenge. In Matthew chapter 5, the Lord Jesus tells us that we are even supposed to love our worst enemies...

43 Ye have heard that it hath been said, Thou shalt love thy neighbour, and hate thine enemy.

44 But I say unto you, Love your enemies, bless them that curse you, do good to them that hate you, and pray for them which despitefully use you, and persecute you;

45 That ye may be the children of your Father which is in heaven: for he maketh his sun to rise on the evil and on the good, and sendeth rain on the just and on the unjust.

46 For if ye love them which love you, what reward have ye? do not even the publicans the same?

If you have to wait until you feel like loving your enemies, you might be waiting an awfully long time.

But if you choose to make a decision to love your enemies, and you allow the Lord to empower you to do so, you may be very surprised at what may happen.

We are supposed to be people of great love. In fact, we were designed to be people of great love.

It should be our goal to radiate love in all that we do. Unfortunately, many people lose sight of what is truly important and get all caught up in the smaller details of what we are supposed to be doing. Even worse, some get so focused on man-made traditions and rules that they completely neglect the core of our faith, which is to love God and to love others.

And before I end this chapter, I don't want anyone to think that I am completely discounting feelings.

It can feel absolutely great to love God and to be loved by God.

And it can feel absolutely great to love others and to be loved by others.

If you immerse yourself in love, you are going to find that you enjoy your life a whole lot more. It is just that we should not be dependent on our feelings. Rather than "following our feelings", good feelings should come naturally as the result of making the right choices and doing the right things.

"I didn't feel like it" is not a legitimate excuse for doing the wrong thing. If we spend our lives being slaves to our emotions, we will end up in a lot of bad places. But if we consistently make good choices based on what the Word of God instructs us to do, we will find that good emotions will often inevitably follow.

And even if making the right decision in the short-term seems painful, there is always a long-term benefit. Loving others is always going to cost us something, and we will continue to explore this in the next chapter...

-CHAPTER FOUR-

"Love Is Far More About What We Do Than It Is About What We Say."

Love is always going to cost something. Even if it is just time and energy, there is a cost to loving someone else.

Just think about your parents for a moment. It would be hard to quantify the vast amounts of money, time and energy that it took to raise you from an infant to an adult. But they invested so much into you because they love you.

Another way of saying this is that love requires a sacrifice. As we discussed in the last chapter, love starts with a decision, and the actions that follow that decision are going to cost you something.

When we hear the word "sacrifice", many of us think of the sacrificial system that we find in the Old Testament. The details of that system can often be difficult for those of us living in modern times to grasp, but it served some absolutely critical purposes.

First of all, the concept that there must be a sacrifice for sin was constantly pounded into the heads of the people in ancient Israel. Every sacrifice foreshadowed the time when the Son of God would come into the world and offer Himself as the sacrifice for the sins of all humanity, and so when that finally happened many Jewish believers instantly understood the doctrine of "atonement" because it was already such a part of their lives.

Today, so many people tend to view God as a kindly old man in the clouds that will just brush our sins under the rug if we feel bad enough about them, but that is not how it works. There is a penalty for sin, and that penalty had to be paid. Because Jesus paid the penalty for all of our sins on the

cross, He is able to offer eternal salvation as a free gift, but that free gift came at a very great cost.

Unfortunately, so many of us tend to be annoyed at even the most minor inconvenience. So getting up early in the morning to read the Bible and pray is not very appealing to a lot of people.

But if we truly want to develop a great love relationship with God, there is no substitute for spending time with Him, and that is going to cost us time and energy that we could be directing toward other endeavors.

And the same thing is true when it comes to loving others. Loving someone else is always going to require some sort of sacrifice, even if it is very small.

That is because true love always requires action. There is certainly nothing wrong with loving others with words, and I actually very much encourage this, but if those words are never followed up by any action they are ultimately meaningless.

Let me share a very clear example of this from the Scriptures. The following is what James 2:15-18 says in the King James version...

15 If a brother or sister be naked, and destitute of daily food,

16 And one of you say unto them, Depart in peace, be ye warmed and filled; notwithstanding ye give them not those things which are needful to the body; what doth it profit?

17 Even so faith, if it hath not works, is dead, being alone.

18 Yea, a man may say, Thou hast faith, and I have works: shew me thy faith without thy works, and I will shew thee my faith by my works.

This is a very powerful passage. Just imagine coming across a homeless person in the community where you live. You can tell that homeless person that you love him or her all day long, but it is the person that actually takes action to help that individual that is showing the most love.

We find a similar principle at work in the story of the Good Samaritan. Take a few moments to consider the words of Jesus in Luke 10:30-37...

30 And Jesus answering said, A certain man went down from Jerusalem to Jericho, and fell among thieves, which stripped him of his raiment, and wounded him, and departed, leaving him half dead.

31 And by chance there came down a certain priest that way: and when he saw him, he passed by on the other side.

32 And likewise a Levite, when he was at the place, came and looked on him, and passed by on the other side.

33 But a certain Samaritan, as he journeyed, came where he was: and when he saw him, he had compassion on him,

34 And went to him, and bound up his wounds, pouring in oil and wine, and set him on his own beast, and brought him to an inn, and took care of him.

35 And on the morrow when he departed, he took out two pence, and gave them to the host, and said unto him, Take care of him; and whatsoever thou spendest more, when I come again, I will repay thee.

36 Which now of these three, thinkest thou, was neighbour unto him that fell among the thieves?

37 And he said, He that shewed mercy on him. Then said Jesus unto him, Go, and do thou likewise.

The story of the Good Samaritan really hits me hard personally, because unfortunately I could see myself responding to the man in need just like the religious leaders in the story did.

For those of us that work really hard and that are on very tight schedules, it can be very difficult to break out of our established patterns to help someone in need. But that is what love is all about. It is about sacrificing something for the benefit of someone else.

Many people equate love and kisses and words of encouragement with love. And all of those can be ways of loving someone, but there are others that may not be very good at physically or verbally expressing love that still love those in their lives very much.

In particular, I am thinking of many fathers that were raised not to show a lot of emotion but that still spent their entire lives trying to provide the very best for their wives and children.

Just because your father was not openly emotional does not mean that he didn't love you very deeply.

If you think back throughout your life, the people that you are probably most grateful for are those that did something for you in a time of great need.

For some people a teacher or a coach was there for them when they needed it the most. For others, it was a family member or a church leader. Love can come from a multitude of directions, and often it can look a lot different from how we would expect it to look.

If you want to be a person of great love, instead of focusing on how you feel about others, try focusing on specific things that you can do to make a measurable difference in the lives of other people.

And sometimes doing the "loving thing" is not an easy choice. In fact, in situations where "tough love" is required, the other party can end up becoming very angry with you.

When someone is engaging in extremely self-destructive behavior, it can be very easy to not say anything and just let that other person do their own thing. But is that love? Of course not. It takes a lot of courage and a lot of love to tell someone that you love very deeply that what they are doing is wrong and to try to get them to change course.

If that individual ends up rejecting you, there is a very real possibility that you could end up with a broken relationship. But if you are successful, the one that you helped could end up being forever grateful for what you have done.

I have a very good friend that is engaged in some extremely self-destructive behavior as I write this book, and I have tried my best to warn him about what could happen to him, and let's just say that he didn't like that very much. So he doesn't want to be my friend anymore, but I will continue to try to help him get turned around because that is the loving thing to do.

Love doesn't just sit back and watch someone destroy themselves and those around them. Love takes action where nobody else will.

And love wants the best for someone else even when they don't want it for themselves.

Another thing about true love is that it is relentless.

I recently came across a tragic story about a woman that had developed a very serious case of thyroid cancer. Because of the nature of her treatment, there were times when she had to be completely isolated from others, but her husband wasn't about to abandon her. He set up a desk right outside of the bedroom where she was resting so that they could still be close to one another all day long as she went through this ordeal. Their daughter was so moved by this gesture that she posted a photo of her father sitting at his desk to Twitter. This story soon went viral and it was picked up by a whole host of mainstream news outlets.

Even if that husband never uttered a single word about how much he loves his wife, we would all know how much he loves her by the grand gesture that he made.

It has been said that life is a series of grand gestures.

If you want to love God greatly, I would encourage you to make some sort of a grand gesture to show Him that.

And if you want to love others greatly, get into the habit of making grand gestures for the benefit of those around you.

In our society today, it can be so easy to be self-absorbed. We have been trained to spend countless hours in front of our televisions and our computers, and as a result most people are deeply lonely.

In such a sea of loneliness, it doesn't take much to make a radical impact. Just sitting down and listening to someone that is hurting for an hour can be incredibly meaningful. Listening is a skill that never goes out of style, and you would be amazed at how people are willing to pour out their hearts if you would just be willing to be quiet and listen for a while.

Have you ever known a selfish person that is truly and deeply happy on a consistent basis? Selfish choices can be gratifying in the short-term, but in the long-term they just bring emptiness and pain.

Our lives are so much more meaningful when we choose to love God and when we choose to love others. But this isn't going to happen by accident. You have got to want to be a person of great love or you will never get there.

God never forces Himself on anyone. If you don't want anything to do with Him or His love, then you are going to get your wish.

You can choose the path of selfishness if you want, but I have tried both ways and I am here to tell you that the path of love is superior by far.

And if you want to be a person that loves, you need to be a person that is action-oriented. Sitting back and meditating on all of the loving feelings that you may have toward someone is not what love is about. Rather, love is about taking action, and of course any action that you take is going to cost you something.

There is a famous song that says that "the best things in life are free", but that is actually not true.

Loving others is always going to require a sacrifice of time, effort, energy, money and lost opportunities.

But the rewards are truly wonderful, and as you grow in love you will soon discover that you are rapidly being transformed into the very best version of yourself.

A lot of people end up regretting not loving others enough once they reach the end of their lives, but nobody ever regrets loving others too much.

-CHAPTER FIVE-

"If You Don't Learn How To Forgive, Every Relationship In Your Life Will Ultimately Fail."

I think that I am going to have to rewrite this portion of the book many times, because this is truly one of the hardest chapters for me to write. The reason why it is so difficult for me to write this chapter is because some terrible things have been done to me, and it was not always easy for me to forgive those that hurt me. And some absolutely horrible things have also been done to people that I love, and sometimes it is even harder to forgive someone that has hurt those you care about than it is to forgive someone that has just hurt you. If you are a parent, then you know exactly what I am talking about.

I have been deeply betrayed by individuals that I loved and deeply trusted. I never imagined that anyone, especially Christian people, could act in such a manner. So if you are struggling with forgiveness, I can identify with you.

When we are feeling deep hurt and pain, there is always a temptation to lash out, but we must resist that temptation. I have forgiven those that have hurt me, and I wish them only the best even though they have never apologized or asked for my forgiveness.

Within the past two years, I have been blindsided by two absolutely shocking betrayals. Both times I was hurt very deeply, and it would have been very easy for me to be seething with bitterness and regret to this day, because in both instances I did absolutely nothing to deserve what happened to me.

It can be very tempting to hold on to the pain and the hurt, because it can feel like you are hurting the other person by refusing to forgive. But the truth is that the only person you are hurting when you refuse to forgive is yourself.

When you hold anger, frustration, bitterness and resentment deep inside, they will eat away at you like a cancer. And in addition to the emotional and spiritual damage that unforgiveness will cause, it can also have a dramatic physical effect on you as well.

According to Johns Hopkins Medicine, studies have found that forgiving others decreases the risk of heart attacks, improves cholesterol levels, makes it easier to sleep, reduces chronic pain, lowers blood pressure, and decreases levels of stress, anxiety and depression.

Alternatively, studies have also found that unforgiveness has the exact opposite effect. If you refuse to forgive, you may very well find yourself soon dealing with heart disease, diabetes or chronic depression.

There are no perfect people, and so no matter how incredible someone may seem at first, eventually that person is going to do something to upset you. And if you do not know how to forgive, it is going to make it very difficult for any interpersonal relationship to last for very long.

So this is why so many people bounce from friendship to friendship, relationship to relationship or even marriage to marriage. Everything can seem great at first, but once something negative happens those that are not willing to forgive will often bail out at the first opportunity.

Any interpersonal relationship can seem wonderful when things are going great, but it is only when a time of testing comes that you discover what you really have.

I received a very hard lesson in this regard fairly recently. Over the course of a year and a half, I developed what I believed was a very strong friendship with someone that I truly respected. But all throughout that time, the friendship was never tested. And of course eventually something did go a bit wrong, and my "friend" immediately turned his back on me and never spoke to me again.

I can't understand never speaking to someone again. In the particular situation that I just described, I didn't even do anything wrong. Of course I tried to reach out to this particular individual but I have never received a response.

We can't control what other people will do, but we can certainly control our own actions.

As for my wife and I, we absolutely refuse to allow any unforgiveness, bitterness or resentment into our lives. That is because we have learned how critical forgiveness is to our spiritual journeys. In Ephesians 4:32 we are specifically commanded to forgive one another...

And be ye kind one to another, tenderhearted, forgiving one another, even as God for Christ's sake hath forgiven you.

And in Matthew 6:14-15, the Lord Jesus makes it very clear how much importance the Father places on our willingness to forgive others...

14 For if ye forgive men their trespasses, your heavenly Father will also forgive you:

15 But if ye forgive not men their trespasses, neither will your Father forgive your trespasses.

There are times when you will need to repeatedly forgive someone because the same offense keeps coming up in your spirit time after time.

When this happens, there are three steps that I like to follow.

First of all, I pray and I tell the Lord that I forgive the other person in the name of Jesus.

Secondly, I let the offense go. It has been said that we should "forgive and forget", but of course if something truly horrible has been done to you it is not likely that it will ever be completely erased from your memory. Instead of trying to "forget", I always tell the Lord that I am willing to "let it go". In other words, I am willing to release whatever pain, anger, frustration and resentment that I have been feeling because of the offense.

Thirdly, I pray that the other party would be blessed. The Scriptures tell us that we are to bless and not curse, and it is very difficult to be angry and resentful when you are blessing someone. As I have discussed previously in this book, we are to even love our worst enemies, and that means that we are to want the very best for them.

Forgiveness can be especially challenging when the other party continues to hurt you over and over again. But according to the Lord Jesus, we are called to forgive others no matter how many times it takes. One of the passages where we find this principle is Matthew 18:21-35...

21 Then came Peter to him, and said, Lord, how oft shall my brother sin against me, and I forgive him? till seven times?

22 Jesus saith unto him, I say not unto thee, Until seven times: but, Until seventy times seven.

23 Therefore is the kingdom of heaven likened unto a certain king, which would take account of his servants.

24 And when he had begun to reckon, one was brought unto him, which owed him ten thousand talents.

25 But forasmuch as he had not to pay, his lord commanded him to be sold, and his wife, and children, and all that he had, and payment to be made.

26 The servant therefore fell down, and worshipped him, saying, Lord, have patience with me, and I will pay thee all.

27 Then the lord of that servant was moved with compassion, and loosed him, and forgave him the debt.

28 But the same servant went out, and found one of his fellowservants, which owed him an hundred pence: and he laid hands on him, and took him by the throat, saying, Pay me that thou owest.

29 And his fellowservant fell down at his feet, and besought him, saying, Have patience with me, and I will pay thee all.

30 And he would not: but went and cast him into prison, till he should pay the debt.

31 So when his fellowservants saw what was done, they were very sorry, and came and told unto their lord all that was done.

32 Then his lord, after that he had called him, said unto him, O thou wicked servant, I forgave thee all that debt, because thou desiredst me:

33 Shouldest not thou also have had compassion on thy fellowservant, even as I had pity on thee?

34 And his lord was wroth, and delivered him to the tormentors, till he should pay all that was due unto him.

35 So likewise shall my heavenly Father do also unto you, if ye from your hearts forgive not every one his brother their trespasses.

Every morning my wife and I start our day by reading the Word of God and praying. And during our prayers, we always make it a point to forgive others. There are certain spiritual disciplines that we all need to make a regular part of our lives, and this is one of them.

In fact, forgiving others is such an important spiritual discipline that the Lord Jesus made it a key component of the Lord's prayer. The following comes from Matthew chapter 6...

⁹ After this manner therefore pray ye: Our Father which art in heaven, Hallowed be thy name.

¹⁰ Thy kingdom come, Thy will be done in earth, as it is in heaven.

¹¹ Give us this day our daily bread.

¹² And forgive us our debts, as we forgive our debtors.

¹³ And lead us not into temptation, but deliver us from evil: For thine is the kingdom, and the power, and the glory, for ever. Amen.

After everything that the Lord has forgiven us for, how could we possibly hold something against someone else?

Once again, I am not suggesting that it is always easy to forgive. We live in a world where just about every type of evil that you can possibly imagine is exploding all around us, and some of the things that are being done to the most vulnerable members of our society are too horrible for words.

There are some people that were abused by others on a consistent basis for many years, and I don't know that I even have the capacity to grasp the horror of what it would be like to go through something like that.

But I also know that with God all things are possible. On our own we may not be able to forgive the horrible things that have been done to us, but God can give us the strength and the power to forgive anything.

And once you choose to forgive, you might just find that the person being let out of prison is you.

When you cling tightly to the pain that someone else has caused you, the truth is that you continue to give that other person power over you. So when you finally let it go, it can feel as though a great weight has been lifted off of your shoulders.

If you choose not to forgive others, the consequences can be dramatic. There are no perfect people, and so everyone in your life is going to let you down at some point. If you never learn how to forgive, you will find that bitterness and resentment toward others are constantly building up in your heart, and every relationship in your life will ultimately fail.

One of the most important keys to having successful relationships with others is being willing to forgive. Yes, there are times when ending a relationship permanently is the wise choice, but even in those situations it is imperative to forgive.

And if you are not willing to forgive others, you might as well forget about the rest of this book. As I stated in the first chapter, all of these principles work together, and leaving a single one out can short circuit the entire system.

There is a reason why the Lord Jesus Christ commands us to forgive others over and over again in the gospels. Long-term human relationships simply do not work without it, and after all of the stuff that God has forgiven us for doing, how could we possibly refuse to forgive what others have done to us?

Love and forgiveness work hand in hand, and if you want to be a person of great love you must also be a person of great forgiveness.

-CHAPTER SIX-

"We Can Change The World."

I am about to get into some of the toughest and most challenging chapters in this book, but before I do I wanted to share some encouraging words. Many people look at the Bible and see a negative message with a long list of rules, but that is not the case at all.

Yes, God does give us instructions, but those instructions are there for our good. They are there for our protection and our provision, and if we follow them we will be blessed and not cursed.

As Americans, we tend to instinctively recoil when someone tries to tell us what to do because we are already overburdened with laws. It has been estimated that if you were to add up all of the laws, rules, regulations and ordinances at all levels of government in the United States that the total would be in the *millions*.

On the other hand, if you count all of the commandments in the Bible the total is only in the *hundreds*.

So which system actually has more freedom?

When we were children, our parents gave us rules, and those rules were for our good. For example, when they told us not to touch a hot burner on the stove, the goal was not to take away our fun. Rather, the purpose was to keep us from a tremendous amount of pain.

So we should be thankful that God has given us instructions for how to live, because life is better when we follow them.

But once again, a relationship with God is not just about following rules. Those that truly know Jesus Christ are able to live with a passion that the rest of the world does not understand. Most people spend their entire lives looking for meaning and purpose, and if they would just turn to the One that created them they could have more meaning and purpose than they ever imagined possible.

As believers, we are building an eternal kingdom that will never pass away, and we are in a life or death battle for the souls of the seven billion people that live on this planet. Even helping a single person find eternal life is greater than anything else we could ever achieve during this lifetime, and once you truly get an eternal perspective on things it changes everything.

Nearly 2000 years ago, Jesus and his small band of followers completely changed the world. At that time much of the known world was dominated by the Roman Empire, and Jesus and his followers lived among a people that were greatly oppressed. They didn't have much money, they certainly weren't famous, and they weren't highly educated.

But they turned the world upside down anyway, and we can do it again.

I would submit that the formula is very simple. This is what 1 Corinthians 13:13 says in the Modern English Version...

So now abide faith, hope, and love, these three. But the greatest of these is love.

That sounds so simple, but faith, hope and love are all in very short supply these days.

First of all, let me talk a little bit about faith. This is a word that has been greatly distorted by many in the Christian world today. Faith is not asking God for a luxury car and then hoping really hard that your wish will come true. Faith is simply believing that what God has said is the truth, and then acting accordingly.

Faith is far more about what you are going to give than it is about what you are going to get, and so we need to get out of this selfish mindset that faith is all about getting our own needs, wants and desires met.

The goal of faith is not to have our will be done. Rather, it is to have His will be done.

And His will is for us to set this world on fire with the gospel of Jesus Christ.

We can change the world - if we will believe.

Sometimes as believers we get caught up in false humility. Many of us like to think that we aren't quite smart enough, or not quite good looking enough, or that we don't have the resources to make a difference in this world.

But God says that all things are possible for those that believe. In Mark 10:27 Jesus tells us the following...

And Jesus looking upon them saith, With men it is impossible, but not with God: for with God all things are possible.

If we will pursue God with all of our hearts, and carefully follow His ways, there is literally nothing that He will not be able to accomplish through us.

And what we have to offer the world is far more valuable than anything anybody else may have to offer.

That is because what we have to offer is the hope of eternal life.

Through Jesus Christ, those we reach can know the life that is truly life, and they can become the people that they were created to be.

And while the rest of the world offers no hope after death, we can offer them the hope of life after death. This hope is talked about in 1 Peter 1:3-5...

3 Blessed be the God and Father of our Lord Jesus Christ, who according to His abundant mercy has given us a new birth into a living hope through the resurrection of Jesus Christ from the dead, 4 to an incorruptible and undefiled inheritance that does not fade away, kept in heaven for you, 5 who are protected by the power of God through faith for a salvation ready to be revealed in the last time.

God has given us everything that we need to be warriors and revolutionaries.

We can set this world on fire for Jesus Christ if we are just willing to surrender all and do things His way.

In fact, in John 12 the Lord Jesus promised us that those that believe in Him would do even greater works than He did during his earthly ministry...

12 Verily, verily, I say unto you, He that believeth on me, the works that I do shall he do also; and greater works than these shall he do; because I go unto my Father.

13 And whatsoever ye shall ask in my name, that will I do, that the Father may be glorified in the Son.

14 If ye shall ask any thing in my name, I will do it.

15 If ye love me, keep my commandments.

16 And I will pray the Father, and he shall give you another Comforter, that he may abide with you for ever;

17 Even the Spirit of truth; whom the world cannot receive, because it seeth him not, neither knoweth him: but ye know him; for he dwelleth with you, and shall be in you.

18 I will not leave you comfortless: I will come to you.

19 Yet a little while, and the world seeth me no more; but ye see me: because I live, ye shall live also.

20 At that day ye shall know that I am in my Father, and ye in me, and I in you.

21 He that hath my commandments, and keepeth them, he it is that loveth me: and he that loveth me shall be loved of my Father, and I will love him, and will manifest myself to him.

Of course many preachers will often quote verse 12 out of context without discussing the rest of the passage.

As you can see, Jesus talks about doing the "greater works" in the context of talking about keeping His commandments. If we do not follow His instructions we might as well forget about the greater works. Walking in holiness is not optional, and I will have much more to say about this throughout this book.

Many people wonder why I talk about sin so much, but there really is no mystery.

Sin is the problem.

If you allow yourself to be trapped by sin, you will never become the person that you were meant to be, and you will never accomplish much of anything for the kingdom of God.

Even in the Church, most people these days are deeply ensnared by sin, and so when you preach about sin and repentance you are preaching freedom and liberty.

Those ministers that refuse to preach about sin and repentance are actually denying people the opportunity to get free. If you can believe it, there are actually high profile preachers that purposely avoid ever using words such as "sin" and "repentance" because they don't want to offend anyone.

But by doing so they are leaving those that are listening to them in an enslaved state, and that is a very cruel thing to do.

Incredibly, many Christians these days cannot even give you a definition of sin because there is so little preaching on it. But those that know their Bibles know that there is a direct definition of sin in the New Testament. This is what I John 3:4 says in the King James Version...

Whosoever committeth sin transgresseth also the law: for sin is the transgression of the law.

Once again, when most Americans see the word "law" they tend to have a negative reaction, but they shouldn't. God's laws are there for our good, and starting with the next chapter we are going to look at this a lot more closely.

All of the Scriptures, from Genesis to Revelation, are God's instruction manual for life, and there is great blessing in following those instructions.

Of course we all have broken God's laws at some point, and that is why Jesus died on the cross. He paid the penalty for our sins so that we would not have to, and now He offers us forgiveness of sins and eternal life as a free gift.

And we have been entrusted with this good news. At the end of the Book of Matthew, Jesus commanded His followers to take this message to the ends of the Earth...

18 And Jesus came and spake unto them, saying, All power is given unto me in heaven and in earth.

19 Go ye therefore, and teach all nations, baptizing them in the name of the Father, and of the Son, and of the Holy Ghost:

²⁰ Teaching them to observe all things whatsoever I have commanded you: and, lo, I am with you always, even unto the end of the world. Amen.

We are literally on a rescue mission. Most of the world is in deep rebellion against their Creator, and we are in a race against time to rescue as many of them as we can.

On our own this is too great a task, and that is why the Lord has given us the Holy Spirit. In our own power we can do nothing, but through the Holy Spirit there is no limit to what can be accomplished.

Once again, I cannot stress enough the immense value of even a single soul. What greater thing could you possibly do for someone than helping that person find eternal life?

If eternal life truly exists, this is the most important issue for every man, woman and child on the entire planet.

And I want you to notice in that very last verse that Jesus tells us that we are to teach those that choose to follow Him that they are to keep His commandments.

A lot of people seem to think that Jesus had different instructions for all of us than His Father did. But of course that isn't true at all. Jesus told us that He and His Father are one (John 10:30), and He stressed that the things that He was telling us came directly from the Father (John 12:49-50).

And Jesus was exceedingly clear that He did not come to get rid of His Father's laws. This is what Matthew 5:17-19 says in the King James Version...

¹⁷ Think not that I am come to destroy the law, or the prophets: I am not come to destroy, but to fulfil.

18 For verily I say unto you, Till heaven and earth pass, one jot or one tittle shall in no wise pass from the law, till all be fulfilled.

19 Whosoever therefore shall break one of these least commandments, and shall teach men so, he shall be called the least in the kingdom of heaven: but whosoever shall do and teach them, the same shall be called great in the kingdom of heaven.

From Genesis to Revelation, the Bible is a single story with a single purpose. And without a doubt, God's instructions are consistent throughout the entire book, and everything in the Scriptures is constantly pointing us to Jesus Christ.

In these last days God is raising up a Remnant that will keep His commandments, that will preach the gospel of Jesus Christ with a passion to the entire world, and that will move in the power of the Holy Spirit like we haven't seen since the Book of Acts.

We know that this Remnant will exist in the last days because the Book of Revelation tells us that it will exist (Revelation 12:17; Revelation 14:12). I will have more to say about this Remnant later in the book.

But for the moment, there are some hard topics that we need to deal with first...

-CHAPTER SEVEN-

"Sex Is Not The Answer."

In our society today, "love" has virtually become synonymous with romantic love, and romantic love has become virtually synonymous with sex.

In other words, the very concept of "love" itself has been greatly twisted, and when you say that word most people are almost immediately going to start thinking of romantic relationships which lead to sex.

This has happened because most of us have been exposed to thousands of hours of television shows, movies, music and other media which continually hammer home this message.

But just because you are in a romantic relationship does not mean that you have love in your life.

Just ask any couple that is on the verge of divorce.

And just because you are having lots of sex does not mean that you have love in your life.

Just ask any prostitute.

Yes, a romantic relationship can be a wonderful source of love and support. But you don't need one to live a life of great love. In fact, I know some single people that are truly living lives of great love and romantic relationships are not even on their radar.

Finding love is not about finding a romantic relationship. Rather, finding love is about loving God with everything that we have inside of us and loving others with the same kind of radical love with which the Lord Jesus loved people.

But without a doubt, romantic love can be a great thing. God was the one that instituted it, and from the very beginning He intended for men and women to fall in love with one another and to enjoy the benefits of romantic love within the confines of marriage.

And when I say "the very beginning", I am not exaggerating. In Genesis 2, we see the concept of marriage being introduced just after the creation of Eve...

21 And the Lord God caused a deep sleep to fall upon Adam, and he slept: and he took one of his ribs, and closed up the flesh instead thereof;

22 And the rib, which the Lord God had taken from man, made he a woman, and brought her unto the man.

23 And Adam said, This is now bone of my bones, and flesh of my flesh: she shall be called Woman, because she was taken out of Man.

24 Therefore shall a man leave his father and his mother, and shall cleave unto his wife: and they shall be one flesh.

And of course I could quote passages all day which show that God forbids sex outside of the institution of marriage. As you will see below, there are very good reasons why He does this.

As I discussed in the last chapter, God's instructions are there for our protection and our provision. There is great blessing inside the boundaries that He has set for us, but when we get outside of those boundaries the consequences can be quite dramatic.

God has not established those boundaries because He wants to take our fun away. On the contrary, God actually wants us to have lives that are full of blessing, life and peace. If we would just listen to Him and follow His instructions, we could avoid a tremendous amount of pain and heartache.

In America today, just about every form of sex other than sex within marriage is being promoted and celebrated. And so most people are running around and having sex with whoever they want, and the results have been absolutely catastrophic.

Right now, the United States has the highest STD infection rate in the entire industrialized world, and according to the Centers for Disease Control there are approximately 20 million new STD cases in the United States every single year.

Overall, approximately 110 million Americans currently have a sexually-transmitted disease.

This is a major national crisis, and yet our leaders are not recommending that people stop having sex outside of marriage. But of course this is the number one thing that could be done to stop the spread of sexually-transmitted diseases.

If all of our young people remained pure until marriage and then only had sex with their spouses after marriage, the spread of sexually-transmitted diseases would be virtually wiped out.

But that isn't going to happen, is it?

It isn't going to happen because almost everyone in our society has decided that they would rather do what they want to do than what God wants them to do. As a result, about 110 million Americans have a sexually-transmitted disease.

Our authorities strongly urge people to practice "safe sex" even though there really isn't such a thing, but at least that would slow down the spread of diseases a little bit.

Of course most people don't want to do that either. USA Today recently reported on a new survey that discovered that an astounding 65 percent of all Americans do not use a condom when they have sex.

When I first came across that number I was absolutely floored. We like to think that we are smartest, most capable and most responsible generation in American history, but the truth is that we are the most foolish.

Another consequence of our "sexual liberty" is a very high rate of unintended pregnancies. Of all the major industrialized nations, we have the highest teen pregnancy rate, but very powerful forces continue to fight very hard to keep abstinence education out of our public schools.

Instead, abortion is heavily promoted as a form of last ditch birth control if other forms fail.

Since Roe v. Wade was decided in 1973, we have murdered approximately 60 million of our own children, and the vast majority of those babies were conceived outside of marriage.

It is a holocaust of unimaginable proportions, and I will have much more to say about this later in the book.

If we would just keep sex where God intended it, things would go so much better for us. God has set before us life and death, blessings and curses, and we just keep on choosing death and curses.

Before I end this chapter, I want to touch on a couple of other hot topics related to sex.

The first one that I wish to address is pornography. Thanks to the Internet, men can now bring pornography into their homes whenever they want, and the result is a national epidemic on an unprecedented scale.

According to the experts, there are now more four million adult websites on the Internet, and they get more traffic than Netflix, Amazon and Twitter combined.

On one of the biggest adult websites, more than 87 billion videos were watched in just one year alone.

If you were to divide 87 billion by the size of the U.S. population, that would break down to about 260 videos watched per person.

And remember, that is just one website out of four million.

It has been reported that close to a third of all Internet traffic now goes to adult websites, and our young people are being exposed to this garbage at a staggering rate. The average high school boy spends about two hours on adult websites every single week, and it has been reported that 83 percent of all boys and 57 percent of all girls in the U.S. have been exposed to group sex while on the Internet.

It is absolutely imperative that parents keep a close eye on what their children are looking at on the Internet, because this stuff is literally destroying millions of young minds.

Sadly, it appears that Christians are consuming as much (or more) pornography as everyone else. In fact, one study found that the Bible Belt is the number one region in the country for pornography consumption.

Other surveys have also found that Christian men are very heavy consumers of pornography. One survey that I often quote discovered that 64 percent of all Christian men in the United States view porn at least once a month, and a different survey discovered that 68 percent of all Christian men in the United States view porn on a "regular basis".

No wonder the church in America is dead.

As long as this is going on, you can forget about revival in the United States. If you are addicted to pornography, you are completely useless for the kingdom of God, and you are in the process of destroying your life.

The good news is that freedom is possible. The Conquer Series is just one of many resources that are designed to help Christian men win the battle over pornography, and if you want to get free I would encourage you to reach out for help.

God didn't create us to be addicted to porn. He created us to live clean, triumphant, passionate lives full of grace, joy and truth, and pornography is a tool that the enemy uses to try to keep us from the good things that God has for us.

If you want to be free, the first step is to get on your knees and start fighting in prayer like you have never fought before. God can help you through this, even if it seems impossible right now.

And you will want to find someone that you can be accountable to. There are ups and downs during any recovery, and having an accountability partner will go a long way toward helping you through those ups and downs.

The second issue that I want to touch on before the end of this chapter is the rise of the LGBTQ community in our society.

Most major surveys have found that while the percentage of Americans that identify as LGBTQ is rising in our society, it is still relatively low.

However, where we are seeing major growth is among our young adults. According to NBC News, one recent survey found that 20 percent of all Millennials now identify as LGBTQ. Other surveys suggest that the level is not quite that high, but everyone agrees that the number of LGBTQ young people is growing steadily.

These days, children even in elementary school are being told that they might be gay. As a result, more young Americans than ever are choosing "alternative lifestyles". For example, according to a study reported on by the New York Post, the percentage of Americans that admit to having engaged in bisexual behavior has more than doubled since 1990.

Just like porn, it can be exceedingly difficult to break an addiction to a sexually immoral lifestyle once you have gone down that path.

But what seems impossible on our own is more than possible when God shows up.

If you doubt this, just go on YouTube and you will find scores of testimonies from people that were once totally enslaved to sexual sin but that now have been completely set free by the blood of Jesus.

Sexual sin is one of the biggest things holding people back from becoming the people that God created them to be. Most churches these days don't address it very much because they want to be careful not to offend anyone. So they preach lots of upbeat and happy messages that keep people coming back week after week, and why that is so important to a lot of these preachers is because that means that the offerings will continue to be large week after week.

But when we don't address the issues that are enslaving people, we rob them of the opportunity to get set free.

All across the United States there are very large churches that are absolutely packed with people that are all chained up by sin. Many of these churches are completely dead, and someday the leadership of those churches will be held accountable for refusing to help people to get free from the things that were enslaving them.

God wants us to live remarkable lives. That is one of the reasons why He has given us His instructions. The Bible is our roadmap, but in order for it to work we have got to be willing to surrender our own agendas and we have got to be willing to do what God wants us to do.

About a decade ago, my wife and I decided that we were going to make a commitment to carefully keep God's commandments, and our lives have never been the same since. I would not be where I am today without doing things God's way, and I am entirely convinced that I would have never had the opportunity to write this book if my wife and I had not made that choice.

The Lord Jesus Christ is offering you a future that is brighter than you can possibly imagine, but you have got to be willing to surrender all and follow His instructions.

My wife and I are praying that you will make the right choice.

-CHAPTER EIGHT-

"A Great Marriage Takes A Lot Of Hard Work."

It has been said that "nothing good in life comes easy". I don't know if that is entirely true, but without a doubt a successful marriage takes commitment, resolve and an enormous amount of hard work. But of course the rewards can be truly great. One survey found that married men are actually more than twice as likely to be "very happy" with life compared to other men. Other surveys have found that married men also tend to be healthier and to make more money, but these facts are not widely publicized.

Instead, popular culture tends to portray marriage as a "ball and chain" that keeps men from having the freedom to run around having sex with as many beautiful women as possible.

And many well-meaning parents actually encourage their children to put off marriage until their educations are complete and until they have established themselves in their new careers.

God always intended for marriage and parenthood to be two of the fundamental building blocks of society, but we decided that we were going to do things our own way. As a result, we have a giant mess on our hands.

In the previous chapter, I discussed the bitter consequences of the "sexual freedom" that so many are enjoying in our day and time, and so I will not repeat those numbers here.

In this chapter, I want to talk about the stunning decline of marriage and family in America today, along with a prescription for how to fix things.

In the early 1970s, around 70 percent of all men in the United States aged 20 to 39 were married. But that number has declined steadily, and now only about 35 percent all men in the United States aged 20 to 39 are married.

These are the years when men should be getting married and starting families, and it just isn't happening. Instead, our culture tells them that there is more happiness in living a single lifestyle, and so men hop from relationship to relationship looking for fulfillment.

According to the Pew Research Center, an astounding 44 percent of Americans between the ages of 18 and 29 now believe that "marriage is becoming obsolete". So instead of getting married, a lot of them just end up living together instead.

In fact, in our society today "living together" is often promoted as a way to "try things out" before permanently committing to marriage. Unfortunately, things don't always work out so well. According to a Brookings Institute study that was recently released "almost half of cohabiting college-educated mothers will break up with their partner before their child turns 12, compared to less than one-fifth of mothers who were married when the child was born".

In other words, "living together" before marriage produces broken families much more frequently.

But no matter what the evidence says, it appears that people are just going to keep doing it anyway. According to the CDC, 74 percent of all 30-year-old women in the United States have cohabitated with a romantic partner without being married, and it has been estimated that 65 percent of all couples that eventually get married live together first.

Of course one of the big reasons why so many young people are so hesitant to get married in the first place is because so many marriages end up failing. The United States has one of the highest divorce rates in the entire industrialized world, and at this point approximately 42 percent of all first marriages in America end in divorce.

In our society almost everything that we buy is disposable these days, and we have come to think of marriage in the same terms.

As long as the romantic feelings are still there and we are still physically attracted to our partners most of us are willing to hang in there, but feelings and physical attraction inevitably fade.

We need to enter into marriage with the mindset that it is a permanent commitment not to be thrown away the moment that we decide that we are no longer happy.

Instead of putting in the hard work necessary for a lifetime commitment, so many in our society would rather enjoy the thrill of finding someone fresh and new when the one that they are with becomes old and boring.

Of course those "serial monogamists" are never happy for long. In fact, most of them are extremely miserable, and many of them end up deeply regretting their lack of permanent commitment once they get older.

Thanks to the factors discussed above, the marriage rate in the United States has now dropped to historic lows.

If you go all the way back to 1920, there were 92.3 marriages a year for every 1,000 unmarried women in the United States.

But today, there are only about 30 marriages a year for every 1,000 unmarried women.

And if you go back to 1950, 78 percent of all households in the United States contained a married couple.

Today, that number is just 48 percent.

God's design is for young people to fall in love, get married and create nurturing homes for the next generation. That is why the destruction of the family is such a big deal. It is the children that suffer the most, and what we are doing to the next generation of Americans is absolutely horrifying.

In 1956, about 5 percent of all babies in the United States were born to unmarried mothers. That means that about 95 percent of all babies were born to women that were married. In those days just about everyone was raised in a home with a father and a mother, and those were good days for America.

But now things have completely shifted. 2008 was the very first year in our history that 40 percent of all babies were born to unmarried mothers, and we have now stayed at that level for eight straight years.

I know some single mothers, and being a single mother is immensely difficult to say the least. God created us so that we all need each other. Mothers need fathers and fathers need mothers, and without a doubt children need both a father and a mother. Of course there are some situations where a parent passes away unexpectedly at an early age, but in most cases our wounds are self-inflicted.

In America today, approximately one out of every three children lives in a home without a father, and in many urban areas the rate is well over 50 percent. This is a national tragedy, and it is something that we desperately need to get fixed.

And the solution is to go back to the way that God originally intended for things to work. As I have discussed in previous chapters, God's instructions are there for our good. If we will just follow what He says, our lives will go so much better.

From the Garden of Eden, God intended for men and women to permanently commit themselves to one another in marriage. We find the following words of Jesus in Matthew 19...

4 And he answered and said unto them, Have ye not read, that he which made them at the beginning made them male and female,

5 And said, For this cause shall a man leave father and mother, and shall cleave to his wife: and they twain shall be one flesh?

6 Wherefore they are no more twain, but one flesh. What therefore God hath joined together, let not man put asunder.

So many people today want to eliminate the differences between men and women, but that is a tragic mistake.

We both have different strengths and weaknesses, and when men and women work together it is a beautiful thing.

Unfortunately, because our society has trashed traditional gender roles we have an entire generation of young men that don't know how to act like men and an entire generation of young women that don't know how to act like women.

Just think about it for a moment. Yes, there are certainly some young men that are responsible, that work hard, and that are more than eager to take on the roles of husband and father.

But way too often young men in America today are irresponsible, sex crazed, beer swilling slackers that have little ambition and would much rather spend time doing "guy things" than spend it serving others.

Where are the servant leaders that are willing to put the interests of their wives and children ahead of their own? In Ephesians 5, the Bible sets a very high standard for husbands...

25 Husbands, love your wives, even as Christ also loved the church, and gave himself for it;

26 That he might sanctify and cleanse it with the washing of water by the word,

27 That he might present it to himself a glorious church, not having spot, or wrinkle, or any such thing; but that it should be holy and without blemish.

28 So ought men to love their wives as their own bodies. He that loveth his wife loveth himself.

29 For no man ever yet hated his own flesh; but nourisheth and cherisheth it, even as the Lord the church:

30 For we are members of his body, of his flesh, and of his bones.

31 For this cause shall a man leave his father and mother, and shall be joined unto his wife, and they two shall be one flesh.

32 This is a great mystery: but I speak concerning Christ and the church.

33 Nevertheless let every one of you in particular so love his wife even as himself; and the wife see that she reverence her husband.

God wants men that are willing to love their wives like Christ loves the church. In Ephesians 5, men are instructed to be willing to die for their wives if that is what is necessary.

If you are a married man and you are reading this, are you ready to die for your wife?

There is so much more that could be said about marriage, but I want to end this chapter with one of the most important keys.

In a previous chapter I talked about the importance of forgiveness, and my wife and I never allow anything to remain unresolved between us. Every couple is going to have conflict at some point, and how you deal with that conflict is going to be one of the primary things that determines how happy your marriage is.

If you are not willing to forgive, your marriage will almost certainly fail. Many couples allow little things to build up for years, and then eventually they have grown so far apart that divorce almost seems inevitable.

Don't let that happen to you. If you feel something building up, go and talk to your spouse about it. Being able to communicate openly and honestly is so critical, and you never want anything to stay unresolved for long.

If both of you will agree that you will never allow unforgiveness, bitterness and resentment in your marriage, that is going to take you a long way.

Of course it also helps greatly if you have a shared set of values. If both of you are moving toward the same target, you will be constantly growing together instead of growing apart.

Personally, my wife is my best friend, and as we both grow closer to God we find that we are also growing closer to each other.

So if you are currently married and you find that your marriage in on rocky ground, you might want to try getting your focus back on God.

The closer you get to Him, the better off your relationship will be.

-CHAPTER NINE-

"Follow The Instructions."

According to a Gallup survey that was released the day before I wrote this chapter, just 24 percent of Americans believe that the Bible is "the literal Word of God". Sadly, this is the lowest figure in the 40 years that Gallup has been asking this question. If you go back to 1976, 38 percent of Americans believed that the Bible is "the literal Word of God".

This shouldn't exactly come as a surprise, because for decades our society has been pushing the Bible out of public life. In colonial America, it was the book that almost everyone based their lives upon, but now it has been virtually erased from most of our lives. In fact, most people live their lives without ever thinking about the Bible much at all.

Looking ahead, things are likely to continue to deteriorate. For Americans under the age of 30, just 12 percent currently believe that the Bible is "the literal Word of God".

We wanted a "secular" system of education, and this is the result.

A different survey by LifeWay Research that was conducted several weeks before the Gallup survey discovered that only 20 percent of all Americans have read through the entire Bible.

Just 20 percent.

This is an absolute tragedy, because the Bible is God's instruction manual for our lives. In this book I have been making repeated references to "God's instructions", and the Bible is where we find those instructions.

Have you ever gotten a new gadget and become frustrated because you can't figure out how it works?

Well, the truth is that you probably didn't bother to read the instruction manual first.

God has given us an instruction manual for life, and when we read it and do what it says our lives will go so much better. God loves us more than we can possibly imagine, and He has given us these instructions for our good. When we willingly choose to disobey His instructions, bad things inevitably happen.

King David was described as a man after God's own heart, and he had a real passion for the Word of God. The longest chapter in the entire Bible was written by David, and virtually every single verse in that chapter is about how good God's instructions are. Psalm 119 is 176 verses long, and I certainly don't have room to reproduce the entire chapter here, but I want to give you a small sample of what you will find if you read the entire thing...

103 How sweet are thy words unto my taste! yea, sweeter than honey to my mouth!

104 Through thy precepts I get understanding: therefore I hate every false way.

105 Thy word is a lamp unto my feet, and a light unto my path.

106 I have sworn, and I will perform it, that I will keep thy righteous judgments.

107 I am afflicted very much: quicken me, O Lord, according unto thy word.

108 Accept, I beseech thee, the freewill offerings of my mouth, O Lord, and teach me thy judgments.

[109] My soul is continually in my hand: yet do I not forget thy law.

[110] The wicked have laid a snare for me: yet I erred not from thy precepts.

[111] Thy testimonies have I taken as an heritage for ever: for they are the rejoicing of my heart.

[112] I have inclined mine heart to perform thy statutes alway, even unto the end.

[113] I hate vain thoughts: but thy law do I love.

[114] Thou art my hiding place and my shield: I hope in thy word.

Do you see what I am talking about?

David loved God's laws, and he was absolutely obsessed with learning them and keeping them. He understood that God is not trying to make us miserable by taking away our fun. Rather, David knew that this was the path to life, love, blessing and peace.

I wish that I had the words to accurately convey how wonderful it is to be walking according to God's instructions. When I was younger, for many years I insisted on doing things my own way, and things didn't work out very well at all. But when my wife and I totally committed ourselves to living God's way, things completely turned around.

So why do people call the Bible "God's Word" in the first place?

Well, the Bible makes this claim about itself. In 2 Timothy 3, we are told the following...

16 All scripture is given by inspiration of God, and is profitable for doctrine, for reproof, for correction, for instruction in righteousness:

17 That the man of God may be perfect, thoroughly furnished unto all good works.

And we find a similar passage in 2 Peter 1...

20 Knowing this first, that no prophecy of the scripture is of any private interpretation.

21 For the prophecy came not in old time by the will of man: but holy men of God spake as they were moved by the Holy Ghost.

The Bible is just not another book that contains stories and wise sayings from people that lived long ago. Rather, it is a love letter that was directly inspired by God, and even though the Lord used a number of different human authors, somehow the Scriptures are a cohesive whole that covers the entire story of human history from the very beginning all the way to the very end.

Of course there are other religious books that also claim to be the Word of God such as the Quran.

So how do we know that the Bible is the correct one?

Well, there have been hundreds of entire books that defend the Bible, and many of them are quite excellent. In this short chapter, I just want to share a few of my favorite points.

One of the primary ways that God self-authenticates His Word is through the use of prophecy. In other words, God has told us how history is going to unfold in advance, and literally hundreds of prophecies in the Bible have already been fulfilled.

Our God is the only God that can tell us the end from the beginning, because there is no one else that can see it all. In Isaiah 46, we are told the following...

⁹ Remember the former things of old: for I am God, and there is none else; I am God, and there is none like me,

¹⁰ Declaring the end from the beginning, and from ancient times the things that are not yet done, saying, My counsel shall stand, and I will do all my pleasure

One of my favorite prophecies in the Bible comes from Psalm 22. In that remarkable chapter, God used King David to compose a graphic portrayal of the crucifixion of Jesus Christ approximately 1000 years before it actually happened. In fact, many Christians don't realize that Jesus even quoted from Psalm 22 while he was hanging on the cross. By doing this, Jesus was pointing out to everyone that the fact that his hands and feet had just been pierced had been prophesied long ago. Incredibly, at the time that Psalm 22 was written crucifixion had not even been invented yet. Here is the most critical portion of Psalm 22 from the King James Version...

¹⁴ I am poured out like water, and all my bones are out of joint: my heart is like wax; it is melted in the midst of my bowels.

¹⁵ My strength is dried up like a potsherd; and my tongue cleaveth to my jaws; and thou hast brought me into the dust of death.

¹⁶ For dogs have compassed me: the assembly of the wicked have inclosed me: they pierced my hands and my feet.

¹⁷ I may tell all my bones: they look and stare upon me.

¹⁸ They part my garments among them, and cast lots upon my vesture.

Another one of my favorite prophecies is the entire chapter of Isaiah 53. Approximately 700 years in advance, God gave the prophet Isaiah specific details about the life, suffering, death and burial of Jesus. Please take a few moments to read over this extraordinary passage...

Who hath believed our report? and to whom is the arm of the Lord revealed?

2 For he shall grow up before him as a tender plant, and as a root out of a dry ground: he hath no form nor comeliness; and when we shall see him, there is no beauty that we should desire him.

3 He is despised and rejected of men; a man of sorrows, and acquainted with grief: and we hid as it were our faces from him; he was despised, and we esteemed him not.

4 Surely he hath borne our griefs, and carried our sorrows: yet we did esteem him stricken, smitten of God, and afflicted.

5 But he was wounded for our transgressions, he was bruised for our iniquities: the chastisement of our peace was upon him; and with his stripes we are healed.

6 All we like sheep have gone astray; we have turned every one to his own way; and the Lord hath laid on him the iniquity of us all.

7 He was oppressed, and he was afflicted, yet he opened not his mouth: he is brought as a lamb to the slaughter, and as a sheep before her shearers is dumb, so he openeth not his mouth.

8 He was taken from prison and from judgment: and who shall declare his generation? for he was cut off out of the land of the living: for the transgression of my people was he stricken.

9 And he made his grave with the wicked, and with the rich in his death; because he had done no violence, neither was any deceit in his mouth.

10 Yet it pleased the Lord to bruise him; he hath put him to grief: when thou shalt make his soul an offering for sin, he shall see his seed, he shall prolong his days, and the pleasure of the Lord shall prosper in his hand.

11 He shall see of the travail of his soul, and shall be satisfied: by his knowledge shall my righteous servant justify many; for he shall bear their iniquities.

12 Therefore will I divide him a portion with the great, and he shall divide the spoil with the strong; because he hath poured out his soul unto death: and he was numbered with the transgressors; and he bare the sin of many, and made intercession for the transgressors.

Remember, all of that was written about 700 years before Jesus was born in Bethlehem.

This passage alone has been responsible for thousands upon thousands of Jewish people coming to know the Messiah in our day and time. It is incredibly difficult to be exposed to this passage and still deny the truth.

7 different times in this chapter, Isaiah tells us that the Messiah will suffer for our sins...

Isaiah 53:4 *Surely he hath borne our griefs, and carried our sorrows*

Isaiah 53:5 *But he was wounded for our transgressions, he was bruised for our iniquities: the chastisement of our peace was upon him; and with his stripes we are healed.*

Isaiah 53:6 *...the Lord hath laid on him the iniquity of us all*

Isaiah 53:8 ...*for the transgression of my people was he stricken*

Isaiah 53:10 *Yet it pleased the Lord to bruise him; he hath put him to grief: when thou shalt make his soul an offering for sin*

Isaiah 53:11 ...*he shall bear their iniquities*

Isaiah 53:12 ...*he bare the sin of many, and made intercession for the transgressors*

In this chapter we are also told that the Messiah would die "with the wicked" and that he would be "with the rich in his death", and that is precisely what happened.

Jesus died alongside thieves, and He was buried in a wealthy man's tomb.

Another remarkable thing about Isaiah 53 was discovered by Bible code researchers. They found that the Hebrew names of Jesus (Yeshua), Mary, Joseph, the names of the 12 disciples, "Messiah", "Galilee", "Passover", "Herod", the term "his cross", the term "let him be crucified" and many other phrases relating to Jesus are literally embedded in the text of Isaiah chapter 53.

Do you think that this is just a coincidence?

One more example that I would like to quickly point out is one of the most complex prophecies in the entire Bible. In Daniel 9:24-27, the prophet Daniel was given a precise timeline for when the Messiah would come, he was told that the Messiah would die "but not for himself", and he was told that all of this would happen BEFORE the Jewish temple was destroyed.

Of course the Jewish temple was destroyed in 70 A.D., and so according to Daniel's prophecy the Messiah had to come before that point in time.

Entire books have been written about the prophecy in Daniel 9, and it is too complex to entirely break down in this chapter, but I just wanted to give you a taste of what is out there.

There is no other God except the one true God, and there is no other book like the Bible. My hope is that what I have shared here will encourage many of you to investigate these things much more.

-CHAPTER TEN-

"Prayer Changes Things."

This is one of the easiest chapters for me to write, because I love to talk about prayer. In the previous chapter, I talked about the Bible, and the primary way that God communicates to us is through His Word. If we really want to get to know God, we need to be in the Scriptures every day, and as we do so our lives will be transformed.

Right along with that, we need to spend time in prayer each and every day. Prayer is the primary way that we communicate with God, and it is a spiritual discipline which has been greatly neglected in our day and time. Yes, most of us are so incredibly busy these days, and so there is not a lot of "extra" time in our schedules.

But if you want to have a great relationship with God, prayer is not optional. And I am not just talking about bowing your head before a meal or a pastor leading a congregation in a few moments of prayer at church. What I am talking about are extended, intimate times spent with God on a consistent basis. It is the things that we do consistently that ultimately determine who we become, and there are very few things that will transform your life more rapidly than consistent prayer.

A lot of people tend to think of prayer as simply rattling off a long list of things that you need to God, and it is true that He wants us to depend upon Him in this way. In Philippians 4:6-7 we are instructed to let our requests be known to the Lord...

6 Be careful for nothing; but in every thing by prayer and supplication with thanksgiving let your requests be made known unto God.

7 And the peace of God, which passeth all understanding, shall keep your hearts and minds through Christ Jesus.

But of course prayer is so much more than that. Some teachers use the acronym "ACTS" to teach on this. "A" is for adoration, "C" is for confession, "T" is for thanksgiving and "S" is for supplication.

Sometimes we tend to focus solely on the supplication part, but we also need to be telling God that we love Him, confessing our sins, and thanking Him for the incredible things that He has done for us.

If my wife and I had not committed ourselves to consistent daily prayer over the years, there is no way that we would be where we are today. Prayer changes things, and this is something that we have seen over and over again.

If you want your circumstances to change, just start praying.

If you want your family to change, just start praying.

If you want your community to change, just start praying.

If you want your nation to change, just start praying.

If we really understood the power of prayer, we would be doing a whole lot more of it. We serve the one true God that created all things, and there is nothing that is out of His reach.

In Matthew chapter 6, Jesus gave us a model for our prayers. It is known as "the Lord's Prayer", and it is very powerful...

9 After this manner therefore pray ye: Our Father which art in heaven, Hallowed be thy name.

10 Thy kingdom come, Thy will be done in earth, as it is in heaven.

11 Give us this day our daily bread.

12 And forgive us our debts, as we forgive our debtors.

13 And lead us not into temptation, but deliver us from evil: For thine is the kingdom, and the power, and the glory, for ever. Amen.

Notice that this prayer begins with a focus on God and it ends with a focus on God.

It can be very easy to slip into throwing up "me-centered prayers", but our prayers are much more powerful when we align our priorities with God's priorities. When we put His will, His kingdom and His purposes first, great things can happen.

Every phrase in the Lord's Prayer is there for a reason. One of the phrases that is often overlooked is "thy kingdom come". For years, I was puzzled as to why that was in there. Yes, Jesus is going to come back someday and establish His kingdom, but if that is inevitable why would God want us to constantly pray about that?

Well, one day I looked up the Greek, and it has a much deeper meaning than that. The word translated in our Bibles as "come" actually means to arise, to come forth, or to go from one place to another.

In other words, it basically means to advance.

So now when I pray that part of the Lord's Prayer, I pray it this way...

"May your kingdom advance, and may your will be done just as it is done in heaven."

We have been given the work of building God's kingdom, and every day we should be praying for a great harvest of souls to come to know the Lord Jesus. There is nothing greater that you can ever do for someone than introducing them to Jesus Christ. The church needs to regain an eternal perspective, because helping others find eternal life is a far greater mission than all of these other plans and programs that we tend to spend so much time, effort and energy on.

The things that I am sharing in this chapter may seem elementary, but when you fully grasp them they will completely revolutionize the way that you look at your life.

One of the things that my wife and I often pray for is that God would make us people of great faith. The Scriptures tell us that without faith it is impossible to please God, and the Lord is looking for people that aren't afraid to ask Him for big things.

Unfortunately, the concept of "faith" has been greatly twisted by many in the Christian world today. There are some ministers out there that are teaching that if you just wish hard enough, God is going to give you whatever you are selfishly desiring at that moment.

But that is not what faith is about at all. The truth is that faith is far more about what you are going to give than it is about what you are going to get, and it begins with lining up with God's commandments. In John 15, Jesus tells us the following...

7 If ye abide in me, and my words abide in you, ye shall ask what ye will, and it shall be done unto you.

Most people immediately skip to the "ask what ye will" part, but first we must abide in Christ and His words must abide in us. That means that we need to spend time with Him, learn what pleases Him, and keep His commandments.

If you are willfully living in sin and purposely choosing not to follow God's ways, you should not expect that God is going to honor your prayers.

Another key element that many miss when they teach on faith and prayer is found in 1 John 5...

14 And this is the confidence that we have in him, that, if we ask any thing according to his will, he heareth us:

15 And if we know that he hear us, whatsoever we ask, we know that we have the petitions that we desired of him.

God is not going to give us answers to our prayers that are contrary to His will.

So all those people that are teaching that God will give you a Ferrari if you just have enough "faith" are not being honest with you.

Unfortunately, a lot of people that get turned off by the abuses in the "faith movement" end up neglecting what the Bible has to say about faith altogether, and that is a tragic mistake. Because if we will line up with God's commandments, walk in holiness and seek to pray in accordance with His will, literally anything is possible. In Mark 9:23, Jesus explained that "all things are possible to him that believeth". And in Ephesians 3:20, the Apostle Paul told us that God "is able to do exceeding abundantly above all that we ask or think".

When I first started writing about a decade ago, I never would have imagined the reach that my work would someday have or the doors that would eventually open up for me. I was just trying to do the best that I could with what I had been given, and I had faith that God had a plan.

In early 2010, my wife and I decided that we would move all the way across the country to start a new life. I was making a little bit of money with my writing at the time, and she was making a little bit of money restoring furniture, and we figured that we could make it somehow. After much prayer and consideration, we moved from the Washington D.C. area to a little town on the outskirts of Seattle called Carnation.

We didn't know if we could make it out there, but we felt that God was calling us to make a big change, and so we stepped out in faith.

When we got to Carnation, Meranda found it more difficult to sell refinished furniture, but fortunately my writing really began to take off. After a little more than a year, we were able to locate and buy a wonderful home in the mountains of Idaho, and we have been here ever since.

Many people would be tempted to think that going from working in the heart of Washington D.C. to living a quiet life in the mountains of Idaho would be a step backwards, but we didn't look at it that way. We prayed, we worked hard and we prepared, and we trusted that God had a great plan for us.

Today, we have reached literally millions of people with our writing, our books, our DVDs and our videos. But God is not done with us yet. We feel like God is now moving us in some exciting new directions, and we can't wait to see what comes next.

But none of these incredible things would have ever happened to us if we had not been committed to prayer and if we had not been willing to trust God for things that many people would have called "crazy" and "unrealistic".

If you study Christian history, you will find that every great move of God always started with prayer. No matter how talented we may be, and no matter how hard we try on our own, God is not going to move unless there are people that are dedicated to seeking Him with all of their hearts.

My wife and I are constantly praying that God would allow us to be on the cutting edge of what He is doing in these last days. We believe that in the midst of all the chaos and all the darkness that are coming that we will also see the greatest move of God that the world has ever seen.

But if we want the fire to fall, we have got to be willing to get on our knees first. Churches that are lukewarm and that have lost their first love should not expect that they are going to see revival. The Scriptures tell us that God is looking for those that will seek Him with everything that they have got (Jeremiah 29:13).

This brings us full circle back to the greatest commandment. In Matthew 22:37, Jesus tells us that the greatest commandment of all is to "love the Lord thy God with all thy heart, and with all thy soul, and with all thy mind". If you ever feel like your life is off course, just start doing that again and everything else will begin falling into place.

God didn't make things complicated. It really is all about loving Him and loving others. So often we get caught up in the smaller details, but in the end the secret to living a great life is actually very simple.

-CHAPTER ELEVEN-

"If You Want To Live A Life That Really Matters, There Is Absolutely No Room For Racism."

I have written about a number of very touchy subjects so far in this book, and I am about to address another. It absolutely astounds me that in America today there are still people that choose to hate others because of the color of their skin. Racism is a great evil, and there is no room for it in our society, and yet we see evidence of it all around us.

In particular, racists like to use the relative anonymity of the Internet to express their vile views. I cannot understand why anyone would want to hate an entire nationality or race, but apparently this is something that is quite widespread. Just spend some time on Facebook, Twitter or Internet discussion forums and you will see exactly what I am talking about.

If we do not learn how to love one another, it is very difficult to see how there could possibly be a positive future for our society.

When you choose to hate someone, you are choosing to hate someone that God created and that He sent His only Son to die on the cross to die for. John 3:16 tells us the following...

16 For God so loved the world, that he gave his only begotten Son, that whosoever believeth in him should not perish, but have everlasting life.

Jesus didn't just die for one race or one nationality. He loves all of us, and He came to die for all of us.

Every single person, no matter how old they are, what they look like or where they are from, is of immense value to God.

So who are you to hate what God loves so deeply?

I think that it helps to remember that every single one of us is in desperate need of God's mercy. Romans 5:8 tells us the following...

8 But God commendeth his love toward us, in that, while we were yet sinners, Christ died for us.

Without Christ, we would all be slaves to sin with absolutely no hope and no future.

But because of Christ, we have been set free from sin and we have a hope and a future that are more glorious than we can possibly imagine right now. Let me share with you just a few verses out of Ephesians 2...

2 Wherein in time past ye walked according to the course of this world, according to the prince of the power of the air, the spirit that now worketh in the children of disobedience:

3 Among whom also we all had our conversation in times past in the lusts of our flesh, fulfilling the desires of the flesh and of the mind; and were by nature the children of wrath, even as others.

4 But God, who is rich in mercy, for his great love wherewith he loved us,

5 Even when we were dead in sins, hath quickened us together with Christ, (by grace ye are saved;)

6 And hath raised us up together, and made us sit together in heavenly places in Christ Jesus:

7 That in the ages to come he might shew the exceeding riches of his grace in his kindness toward us through Christ Jesus.

8 For by grace are ye saved through faith; and that not of yourselves: it is the gift of God:

9 Not of works, lest any man should boast.

After the grace that we have been shown through Christ, how can we possibly hold on to hatred for others?

We were all created by God, and we are all dependent upon God for every single breath that we take. What we have in common vastly outweighs any other considerations, and this was reflected by our founders in the Declaration of Independence...

We hold these truths to be self-evident, that all men are created equal, that they are endowed by their Creator with certain unalienable Rights, that among these are Life, Liberty and the pursuit of Happiness.

One of the reasons why racism flourished during the 18th, 19th and 20th centuries was because western society began to forget that we all came from the same Creator. Instead, many began to embrace the theory of Darwinian evolution, and that theory often leads many to the conclusion that some humans are "superior" or "more evolved" than other humans. During the 20th century in particular, we witnessed the endgame of that sort of thinking, and the millions upon millions of deaths should have shocked the world into realizing how morally bankrupt the theory of evolution really is. But instead the theory of evolution is more popular globally than ever before, and that has very frightening implications for our future.

Ultimately, the secret to ending racism is the same secret that I have been sharing all throughout this book.

It is all about loving God and loving others.

If we truly love God, we aren't going to continue to hate the people that He greatly loves.

And if we commit ourselves to truly loving others, there is not going to be any room for racism.

I have never met a great man or woman of God that is racist, and I never will. God loves everyone, and that needs to be our heart as well.

I would like to conclude this chapter by sharing with you the ending of Dr. Martin Luther King Jr.'s famous "I Have A Dream" speech. These words have stuck with me throughout my entire life, and I believe that they paint a picture of what America could be like someday if we all truly learn how to love one another...

And so let freedom ring from the prodigious hilltops of New Hampshire.

Let freedom ring from the mighty mountains of New York.

Let freedom ring from the heightening Alleghenies of Pennsylvania.

Let freedom ring from the snow-capped Rockies of Colorado.

Let freedom ring from the curvaceous slopes of California.

But not only that:

Let freedom ring from Stone Mountain of Georgia.

Let freedom ring from Lookout Mountain of Tennessee.

Let freedom ring from every hill and molehill of Mississippi.

From every mountainside, let freedom ring.

And when this happens, and when we allow freedom ring, when we let it ring from every village and every hamlet, from every state and every city, we will be able to speed up that day when all of God's children, black men and white men, Jews and Gentiles, Protestants and Catholics, will be able to join hands and sing in the words of the old Negro spiritual:

Free at last! Free at last!

Thank God Almighty, we are free at last!

-CHAPTER TWELVE-

"Respect Life."

It is no longer okay for Republican politicians to claim that they are Pro-Life during their campaigns but then vote to fund Planned Parenthood while they are in office. As a conservative voter, I have been extremely frustrated by supposedly "conservative" politicians that think that it is okay to betray the Pro-Life movement over and over again. More specifically, I cannot understand how any "Pro-Life" politician could possibly vote to give Planned Parenthood approximately 500 million dollars in federal funding year after year.

It is time for conservative voters to take matters into their own hands. In 2018, conservatives will be the deciding factor in Republican primaries all over the nation. If we work together and stand strong, we could ensure that the vast majority of Republican candidates for office in 2018 are truly Pro-Life.

So what I am suggesting is that we require all Republican candidates for office to take a pledge to always vote against any bill that gives even a single penny of funding to Planned Parenthood. This would apply on the federal, state and local levels. We would let them know that if they are not willing to pledge that there will be no money for Planned Parenthood under any circumstances that we will not vote for them under any circumstances.

And just because someone is running as an incumbent does not mean that they would get a pass. If a Republican incumbent will not take the pledge, we will find someone to run against that incumbent who will.

If we actually did this, we could virtually assure that Planned Parenthood would be defunded. The Republicans are very likely to remain in control of the House of Representatives again in 2018, and any bill to fund Planned Parenthood has to get the approval of the House. If we were to pack the House with conservatives that would never vote for any bill that funds Planned Parenthood, there is nothing that the Senate or the White House could do to override that.

This can actually happen, but we have to be united. And all that we would require would be one simple pledge:

"I will not vote in favor of any bill that includes funding for Planned Parenthood under any circumstances."

This is my stand, and I am not moving from it. Any candidate that does not make this pledge will not get my support or my vote.

Since Roe v. Wade was decided in 1973, close to 60 million babies have been slaughtered in America's abortion mills. We are killing children on an industrial scale, and yet most Americans have accepted this as "normal".

And Planned Parenthood is the biggest offender by far. Planned Parenthood performs more than 300,000 abortions every year, and they get more funding from the federal government than any other source by a very wide margin.

By giving Planned Parenthood about half a billion dollars a year, the United States government is putting a giant stamp of approval on what Planned Parenthood is doing. Of course none of that money is actually supposed to be used to provide abortions, but everyone knows what the real deal is.

Planned Parenthood is in business to provide abortions. In fact, former Planned Parenthood workers have revealed that they actually had to try to meet "abortion sales quota goals" each month. If the quotas were met, workers were rewarded with pizza parties and other incentives. The following testimony comes from former Planned Parenthood center manager Sue Thayer...

"It was on this big grid, and if we hit our goal, our line was green. If we were 5 percent under it was yellow, if we were 10 percent under it was red. That's when we needed to have a corrective action plan – why we didn't hit the goal, what we're going to do differently next time," she said.

"So we were really very goal-oriented. I trained my staff the way that I was trained, which was to really encourage women to choose abortion, to have it at Planned Parenthood, because that counts toward our goal."

(http://www.wnd.com/2017/02/video-planned-parenthood-insiders-confirm-abortion-quotas/)

Yes, this is really taking place in America today.

Workers are actually being given incentives to convince women to kill their own children.

Even more alarming is the harvesting of body parts that is going on at Planned Parenthood clinics nationwide.

Even though it is a violation of federal law, aborted babies are being chopped up and their organs are being sold off to the highest bidder. This is the kind of thing that you would have expected to see in Nazi Germany, but instead it is actually happening in the United States of America in our day and time.

The Center for Medical Progress has released undercover video after undercover video documenting that this is being done, and yet only a small segment of the population has expressed outrage.

In one of the most recent videos, a Planned Parenthood executive is shown "haggling over per-specimen pricing for livers, lungs, and brains"...

New undercover video shows Dr. Mary Gatter, the Planned Parenthood senior executive who infamously laughed "I want a Lamborghini" about payments for aborted fetal parts, again haggling over per-specimen pricing for livers, lungs, and brains, even while insisting the purchaser must do all the work to harvest.

(http://www.centerformedicalprogress.org/2017/04/2027/)

In another undercover video, a Planned Parenthood doctor in Texas discussed what she would do to babies in their second trimester so that their heads would come out "pretty intact" for harvesting...

The eleventh video release from The Center for Medical Progress in the ongoing Planned Parenthood baby parts scandal shows the abortion doctor for Planned Parenthood in Austin, TX, Dr. Amna Dermish, describing a partial-birth abortion procedure to terminate living, late-term fetuses which she hopes will yield intact fetal heads for brain harvesting.

Dr. Dermish admits she was trained by the Senior Director of Medical Services at Planned Parenthood Federation of America, Dr. Deborah Nucatola. Nucatola described a partial-birth abortion technique to harvest fetal organs in the first Planned Parenthood video released July 14 by CMP.

***"My aim is usually to get the specimens out pretty intact,"** says Dermish, speaking to actors posing as a fetal tissue procurement company. Dermish admits that she will sometimes use ultrasound guidance to convert a 2nd-trimester fetus to a feet-first breech presentation:*
"Especially the 20-weekers are a lot harder versus

the 18-weekers, so at that point I'll switch to breech."

(http://www.centerformedicalprogress.org/2015/10/planned-parenthood-tx-doc-harvesting-intact-fetal-heads-will-give-me-something-to-strive-for/)

How can our "Pro-Life politicians" possibly fund this kind of evil?

When is enough going to be enough? How far do things have to go before we say "**NO MORE**"?

This isn't just another political issue. This is a battle for the soul of our nation. If we continue to allow this to go on, and the federal government continues to give hundreds of millions of dollars to the organization that is doing this, there is no future for our country.

I am not exaggerating one bit when I say that.

When you total up all forms of abortion, including abortion drugs such as RU 486, more than a million abortions are performed in the United States every single year.

To put that in perspective, the number of American children killed by abortion **each year** is roughly equal to the number of U.S. military deaths that have occurred in the entire history of our nation.

Or let us look at this another way. The number of Americans being aborted **each day** is roughly equal to the number of victims that died during the destruction of the World Trade Center towers on 9/11.

In other words, it is like a new 9/11 each and every single day of the year.

If we are truly Pro-Life, we have got to do something to stop this. Many have pinned their hopes on overturning Roe v. Wade, but even if that happened tomorrow that would not outlaw abortion. Instead, each state would be able to make their own laws about abortion, and most of the larger states such as California and New York would continue to keep it legal.

Yes, let us try very hard to continue to get more Pro-Life justices on to the Supreme Court. In fact, if I end up in Congress I will work very hard to see that happen. But we can make much more of an immediate impact by going after Planned Parenthood. If we can get Planned Parenthood defunded on the federal level, it would be absolutely devastating for them, and it is likely that many clinics around the country would have to start closing down.

By the age of 45, approximately one out of every three women in the United States will have had an abortion, and close to half of all women that get an abortion each year have had one before.

We have created a culture of death, and in some areas of the country abortion rates are so high that it is hard to believe that the numbers are actually true.

For example, it has been reported that 41 percent of all New York City pregnancies end in abortion, and according to Pastor Clenard Childress approximately 52 percent of all African-American pregnancies in the entire nation now end in abortion.

And most of the women that are getting abortions in the United States claim to be Christian.

Yes, this is actually true. According to Operation Rescue, Protestant women get 42 percent of all abortions and Catholic women get 27 percent of all abortions.

We are a "Christian nation" that has murdered nearly 60 million of our own children, and close to 90 percent of those murders were performed "for the sake of convenience".

Either abortion is murder or it isn't.

If it is murder, how can any self-respecting "Pro-Life" politician ever vote to give federal funding to an organization that is murdering more than 300,000 American children a year?

And there is really good money in murdering children these days. In fact, 30 Planned Parenthood executives make more than $200,000 a year, and a few of them actually make more than $300,0000 a year.

The blood of tens of millions of precious little children is crying out from the ground against us, and yet most of our politicians just continue on with business as usual.

And of course the United States is far from alone. Since 1980, more than a billion children around the world have been aborted.

Just think about that for a moment.

What do you think God thinks about a billion dead babies?

There are some people out there that are suggesting that the United States is heading for a period of great blessing despite the fact that we have killed close to 60 million of our own children and we continue to kill them on an industrial scale every single day.

It doesn't work that way.

If we want to have any hope of turning this nation around at all, we have got to quit slaughtering children.

So I don't have any more patience for politicians that want to use the Pro-Life label to get votes but then are willing to hand Planned Parenthood hundreds of millions of our tax dollars every year once they get into office.

If you vote to fund Planned Parenthood, you are not Pro-Life.

It really is that simple.

In 2018, let us choose not to compromise any longer. If a candidate will not promise to deny funding to Planned Parenthood, we will deny them our votes.

Personally, this is my line in the sand, and I am not moving.

-CHAPTER THIRTEEN-

"Become like a child."

One of the secrets to living a great life is to never lose your inner toddler. That may sound strange, but just stick with me for a few minutes. In the Modern English Version of the Bible, this is how the first five verses of Matthew 18 read...

At that time the disciples came to Jesus, saying, "Who is the greatest in the kingdom of heaven?"

2 Jesus called a little child to Him and set him in their midst, 3 and said, "Truly I say to you, unless you are converted and become like little children, you will not enter the kingdom of heaven. 4 Therefore whoever humbles himself like this little child is greatest in the kingdom of heaven. 5 And whoever receives one such little child in My name receives Me.

In this passage Jesus tells us that we need to "become like little children". As adults we can be so incredibly pretentious, but throughout the gospels Christ is constantly stressing the need to humble ourselves. This is incredibly tough to do, because society trains us to do the exact opposite.

But children instinctively know that they are completely and utterly dependent on their parents, and that is exactly how we need to be with God. If we try to do things in our own strength and our own power we will fail, but when we depend on the One who created all things we quickly discover that all things are possible.

When I was a young man, it felt good to be filled with pride. I had elaborate plans for my life, and I wanted to show everyone how great I could become. But of course God was not pleased with that approach at all. In 1 Peter 5:5, we are told that God actually resists the proud...

God resisteth the proud, and giveth grace to the humble.

Do you want God to resist you?

That certainly does not sound like a recipe for success, and I found that out the hard way. Over the course of time God humbled me greatly, and as I described in the first chapter I ultimately came to a very low point in my life.

But sometimes it is at our lowest points that the greatest things happen.

I learned the value of humility. I learned that I must surrender all of my plans and all of my programs to God, and that I must trust that His will is much better than my will.

One of the things that my wife and I constantly pray now is this...

Not my will, may your will be done. Less of me and more of you.

If you incorporate just those two phrases into your prayer life, you will start seeing dramatic changes.

When we choose to humble ourselves, God often responds in amazing ways. For example, James 4:10 tells us the following...

Humble yourselves in the sight of the Lord, and he shall lift you up.

So if we are prideful the Lord will resist us, but if we humble ourselves the Scriptures promise us that He will lift us up.

And ultimately that is what happened in my case. As my wife and I completely surrendered ourselves to God's plan, the most remarkable things began to happen. Doors started to open that we never dreamed could possibly open, and we started to live an overflowing life that was far beyond anything that we could have ever imagined planning for ourselves.

All of us need to understand that every single good thing that we have in our lives is from God. When things go well for any of us, it is absolutely imperative that we always give Him the glory. Because the truth is that we could not take another breath without Him. Every single moment is a gift from above, and the moment any of us start drifting off into pride we are going to get into deep trouble.

In Proverbs 9:10, we are told that "the fear of the Lord is the beginning of wisdom". This isn't the kind of fear that causes you to run away, but rather it is about being consumed with awe, reverence and humility. We are to see Him as He truly is, and we are to see ourselves as we truly are.

If it wasn't for God, none of the good things that have happened in my life would have ever taken place. In fact, without the Lord Jesus Christ I believe that I would probably be dead today. So I am not ashamed to give God all of the credit and all of the glory for all of the remarkable things that He has done in and through my wife and I.

He is not just part of our life.

He is our life.

Humility is one of those spiritual disciplines that we need to be practicing every day. It is not just a one time thing where you humble yourself and then you can forget about it. If you truly want to live a life that really matters, you have got to make a habit of humbling yourself.

And any time you need a picture of what that looks like, just spend some time around a little child. One of the reasons why little children are so special is because they haven't learned how to be pretentious yet. They haven't learned how to put on all of the masks that adults do, and so they are often much more fun to spend time around than adults are.

It is time to take the masks off and to lay our souls bare and to acknowledge that we are nothing without the One who created us. If it wasn't for Him, we would have absolutely no hope and no future, but because of Him we have a future that is greater than we could possibly imagine right now.

It is not about you, and it is not about me.

Rather, it is all about Him.

There will be other chapters in this book that are longer, but this is one of the most important. Whenever you feel yourself starting to drift off track, just keep coming back to this secret. Humble yourself, surrender everything to God, and ask Him to help you with whatever you are going through.

We serve a God of miracles, and no matter how bad things may seem right now, there is always a way back.

-CHAPTER FOURTEEN-

"The joy of the Lord is your strength."

Have you ever known someone that has completely lost all joy? Sadly, this sometimes happens as people start to get older. No matter what is happening or who is around, there are some elderly people that have decided to respond to everything with anger and bitterness. It is almost as if the life has totally been sucked out of them.

But that is not how we are supposed to live. Just think about it. How many toddlers have you ever known that are constantly angry and bitter? It just doesn't happen, because they were not made that way.

We have to learn to give up our joy. My daughter is just over two years old right now, and she is able to find joy in just about everything. When we pull up to the park or one of her favorite Sesame Street programs comes on, the joy on her face is undeniable. And sometimes she has a loud outburst of joy for seemingly no reason whatsoever.

When I watch my young daughter, I am reminded of the way that I am supposed to be. I am not supposed to be bitter and jaded and cranky. Instead, I am supposed to squeeze as much out of life as I possibly can, and I am supposed to find the joy in each and every circumstance.

And before I go any further, I want to make a distinction between happiness and joy. Happiness is something that is externally triggered, and it can come and go quite frequently. But the kind of joy that we see described in the Bible is a deeper attitude of the heart. Because we know who we are, what our purpose is and what our ultimate destination is, we can have great joy even in the midst of horrible trials. In fact, in the Scriptures we often see joy and trials discussed together. For example, the following is what James 1:2-4 says in the New International Version...

2 Consider it pure joy, my brothers and sisters, whenever you face trials of many kinds, 3 because you know that the testing of your faith produces perseverance. 4 Let perseverance finish its work so that you may be mature and complete, not lacking anything.

Are we really supposed to experience joy when people are persecuting us for what we believe?

According to the Bible, the answer is yes. And the reason that we can do this is because we are looking forward and not behind. This is what 1 Peter 1:3-9 tells us...

3 Blessed be the God and Father of our Lord Jesus Christ, which according to his abundant mercy hath begotten us again unto a lively hope by the resurrection of Jesus Christ from the dead,

4 To an inheritance incorruptible, and undefiled, and that fadeth not away, reserved in heaven for you,

5 Who are kept by the power of God through faith unto salvation ready to be revealed in the last time.

6 Wherein ye greatly rejoice, though now for a season, if need be, ye are in heaviness through manifold temptations:

7 That the trial of your faith, being much more precious than of gold that perisheth, though it be tried with fire, might be found unto praise and honour and glory at the appearing of Jesus Christ:

8 Whom having not seen, ye love; in whom, though now ye see him not, yet believing, ye rejoice with joy unspeakable and full of glory:

9 Receiving the end of your faith, even the salvation of your souls.

Those that do not know Christ cannot understand this kind of joy, because all they have to look forward to is this life. If something comes along that takes away the future that they thought they were supposed to have, it can be extremely difficult for them to ever find much joy again.

But we have a future that is glorious beyond imagination, and nobody can ever steal or destroy it.

That is a good reason to have joy!

On top of that, there is also great joy in serving God and communing with Him in the here and now. In Psalm 16:11, we are told that there is tremendous joy in being in God's presence...

Thou wilt shew me the path of life: in thy presence is fulness of joy; at thy right hand there are pleasures for evermore.

If you are ever feeling down, just put on some great praise and worship music. It might take a while, but eventually you will find your mood starting to turn around.

It is extremely hard to stay depressed when you are in the presence of God. The most wonderful times I have had with music in my entire life have been when I have been praising and worshiping God. The Scriptures tell us that praise and worship literally invite the presence of God, and when God shows up it changes everything.

One of the things that really frustrates me is when I go to a church worship service and the people there are not really into it. As I discussed earlier in this book, the Bible tells us that we should love the One that created us with everything that we have inside of us. If we are to love Him with all of our heart, all of our soul, all of our mind and all of our strength, somewhere along the way that is going to involve some emotion.

In Psalm 47:1, we are instructed to "shout unto God with the voice of triumph", and in Philippians 4:4 we are told to continually rejoice...

Rejoice in the Lord always: and again I say, Rejoice.

Have you ever known someone that just seems to be bursting with joy? They are infectious, and people want to be around them. I know that I certainly love to be around people that are truly joyful.

But what about people that have no joy? Do you want to spend time with people like that?

Of course not. Being around people that have had all of the joy sucked out of them can be incredibly draining.

When we radiate joy, we reflect who Jesus is to a lost and dying world.

So seek to cultivate joy, because living in joy will make you a light in a world that is filled with darkness.

-CHAPTER FIFTEEN-

"Never lose your sense of wonder."

This is another area that comes so naturally to little children. When I watch my two-year-old daughter play, it amazes me how she is fascinated by every little thing. She absolutely loves to learn, and she has a sense of wonder about everything around her that is almost palpable.

Somewhere along the way, most of us lose this sense of wonder that we had as a child. In fact, many of us end up giving up on learning altogether. Some do it once they leave school, others do it once they retire, and for others they simply get to a point where they don't want to put in the effort any longer.

But when you stop learning, you stop growing as a person. We all know people that have fallen into this trap, and we do not want to allow this to happen to us. We want to always be expanding our horizons and taking on new challenges. In fact, many of the greatest heroes that we admire throughout history had their greatest achievements near the end of their lives.

My wife and I believe that the greatest chapters of our lives are still ahead of us, and that gives us something to look forward to. We never want to become so set in our ways that we close ourselves off to a new adventure that might be just around the corner.

Of course the greatest source of knowledge and wisdom is God's Word. Even if you have read the entire Bible hundreds of times, the Bible can still speak to you in fresh and exciting ways every single day. Those that have been immersed in the Word of God for many years know exactly what I am talking about.

Just a few days ago, I was so excited to point out a verse in Ezekiel to my friend Robert that I had never really noticed before. I had read over that passage in Ezekiel countless numbers of times, but because of my current circumstances this particular verse spoke to me in a way that I had never encountered previously.

One sign of spiritual maturity is a hunger for the Word of God, and this is one of the things that made King David a man after God's own heart. Psalm 119 is the longest chapter in the entire Bible, and in this chapter King David speaks over and over again about how much he loves God's Word. For example, in Psalm 119:71-73 David's great passion for learning God's ways comes through very clearly...

71 It is good for me that I have been afflicted; that I might learn thy statutes.

72 The law of thy mouth is better unto me than thousands of gold and silver.

73 Thy hands have made me and fashioned me: give me understanding, that I may learn thy commandments.

Many people may consider it to be a waste to spend time reading the Bible every day, but I would never be where I am today without doing it. The Bible is God's blueprint for an overflowing life, and there is great blessing in following what it says. The following is how Psalm 1 begins...

Blessed is the man that walketh not in the counsel of the ungodly, nor standeth in the way of sinners, nor sitteth in the seat of the scornful.

2 But his delight is in the law of the Lord; and in his law doth he meditate day and night.

3 And he shall be like a tree planted by the rivers of water, that bringeth forth his fruit in his season; his leaf also shall not wither; and whatsoever he doeth shall prosper.

The reason why I know that this promise is literally true in our day and time is because I have seen the evidence in my own life.

As I have discussed repeatedly in this book, God's instructions are there for our good. If we will follow them, they will lead us to blessing, life and peace. If we reject them, we set ourselves on a path that leads to just the opposite.

We never want to get to the point where we think that we know it all. No matter how much you think you may know right now, I guarantee you that there is still so much more to learn.

I have found that those that are truly wise are those that realize how little they actually know. It can be quite humbling when you finally realize how limited we truly are as humans, and just when we think that we have everything figured out God can turn our worlds upside down in a single moment.

There is always another page to turn, and there are always more adventures to discover. So let's quit being so proud and so jaded, and let's learn to truly cultivate a sense of wonder.

And just like little children, we can even do this with the small things. The other day, I told my wife that an NBA Finals game that I had just watched between Golden State and Cleveland was some of the most beautiful basketball that I had ever seen in my entire life, and in that moment I was expressing my inner sense of wonder. That is something that I need to do a lot more often.

We should never be afraid to embrace the "wow moments" in our lives. If you ever get to the point where you never say "wow" about anything anymore, then that is a major red flag.

One of the first words that my daughter learned was "wow", and now she uses it all the time. And if she gets really excited about something, she will sometimes just start uttering a string of "wows".

That is how I want to be. I want to be in awe of this incredible world that God has created and in awe of the extraordinary things that the people that He has created are doing in it.

Our world is such an amazing place, and we are truly blessed to be living at this moment in history. Personally, my wife and I are so glad that we got to live right here and right now. All of human history has been building up to this time, and we are going to get to see and experience things in this generation that nobody else has ever gotten to see and experience.

There will always be great challenges, but we should never be afraid of what the next chapter of our lives will bring, because the next chapter might just be the greatest one of all.

-CHAPTER SIXTEEN-

"Don't stop believing."

Until you are dead and in the ground, there is always a way to turn things around. This is a belief that I have clung to my entire life, and it has gotten me through some pretty dark times. At this moment it may appear that there is absolutely no hope for you, but I assure you that there is. Everybody gets knocked down in life, but those that choose to have faith are able to keep getting back up.

When I was growing up, a song by Journey entitled "Don't Stop Believin'" was a great source of inspiration to me. The lyrics of the song don't make a whole lot of sense, but that didn't matter at the time. What mattered is that the song inspired me to keep on fighting even when it didn't look like there was still any reason to fight.

During the darkest days of World War II, Great Britain felt all alone in the fight against Nazi Germany, and it looked like all hope was lost. But no matter how long the odds appeared to be, Winston Churchill and other brave British leaders refused to quit.

Not too long after the war started to take a turn for the better, Churchill delivered one of his most famous speeches. In this particular speech to a group of students, he explained that after everything that Great Britain had just been through, the main lesson that he learned was to never give in no matter how dire the situation may appear to be at the time...

You cannot tell from appearances how things will go. Sometimes imagination makes things out far worse than they are; yet without imagination not much can be done. Those people who are imaginative see many more dangers than perhaps exist; certainly many more than will happen; but then they must also pray to be given that extra courage to carry this far-reaching imagination. But for everyone, surely, what we have gone through in this period—I am addressing myself to the School—surely from this period of ten months this is the lesson: never give in, never give in, never, never, never, never-in nothing, great or small, large or petty—never give in except to convictions of honour and good sense. Never yield to force; never yield to the apparently overwhelming might of the enemy. We stood all alone a year ago, and to many countries it seemed that our account was closed, we were finished. All this tradition of ours, our songs, our School history, this part of the history of this country, were gone and finished and liquidated.

(http://www.preachingtoday.com/illustrations/2003/januar y/14163.html?start=2)

This is the kind of faith that God wants us to have. It is easy to have faith when everything is going great, but what God is looking for is faith that refuses to quit even when it looks like all hope is lost.

In fact, Hebrews 11:6 tells us that without faith it is impossible to please God at all...

But without faith it is impossible to please him: for he that cometh to God must believe that he is, and that he is a rewarder of them that diligently seek him.

One of the key differences between those that live lives that really matter and those that don't is simply a willingness to keep going. There are going to be times when we are all tempted to give up. Richard Nixon, Jimmy Carter, Ronald Reagan, Bill Clinton, George W. Bush and Barack Obama all lost important elections early in their political careers, and they could have chosen to completely give up after those losses. But they all kept going, and they all eventually became president of the United States.

There are times when God takes His people to the limit. It is easy to have "faith" when it seems like everything is coming up rainbows and unicorns, but it takes another type of faith entirely when the road is long and you are hanging on by your fingernails.

And James 1:2-4 tells us that we should be thankful for the testing of our faith, because the testing of our faith produces spiritual maturity in us...

2 Consider it pure joy, my brothers and sisters, whenever you face trials of many kinds, 3 because you know that the testing of your faith produces perseverance. 4 Let perseverance finish its work so that you may be mature and complete, not lacking anything.

Perhaps you are at one of the lowest points of your entire life as you read this book.

Some of you may even be considering suicide.

Don't do it. No matter how bad things are at this moment, God can take the broken pieces of your life and turn them into a beautiful thing.

A decade ago, if someone would have told my wife and I all of the wonderful things that God was going to do in our lives over the next ten years we would have laughed at them. But we did have enough faith to believe that God had a wonderful plan for our lives and that we needed to keep fighting.

So we kept going when we were working meaningless jobs that we didn't enjoy at all.

So we kept going when we were deep in debt with seemingly no way out.

So we kept going through all of the aches, pains, setbacks and heartbreaks.

So we kept going when nobody else out there believed in us.

And after all of the miracles that have already happened, we have the audacity to believe that the greatest chapters of our lives are still ahead of us.

If everybody else thinks that we are crazy, we don't care, because we know whom we have believed, and we are persuaded that He can do exceedingly abundantly beyond all that we ask or imagine.

At so many points along the way, my wife and I could have given up on our crazy dreams, but we didn't.

And so now by the grace of God we are living lives that really matter.

You can live a life that really matters too - but you have got to be willing to keep fighting.

So don't stop believing, because God is not done with you yet.

-CHAPTER SEVENTEEN-

"Do not despise small beginnings."

It has been said that a journey of a thousand miles begins with a single step. Well, I would like to share a little bit of my own journey with you, and hopefully this will inspire someone out there. I have previously shared this on *The Economic Collapse Blog,* but I also wanted to share this here. So many people are afraid to try to make a difference because they don't believe that they could make much of an impact. But I am here to tell you that you can make an impact, even if you start very, very small.

We live in a day and age when you don't have to be a celebrity to make a difference. I know this is true because ten years ago I was about as anonymous as you could possibly get. I was newly married and working as a lawyer in the heart of Washington D.C. not too far from the White House. That may sound glamorous to you, but it definitely was not. Approximately one out of every 12 residents of D.C. is a lawyer according to some estimates, and so they are a dime a dozen. And my work was about as meaningless as you could get. If there was a lawyer version of a toilet scrubber, that would have been me. Nobody knew who I was, and nobody cared who I was. I was having no real measurable impact on the world around me, but I wanted to. I just didn't know how.

In 2008, I started to look into something called blogging. I learned that there were more than a million blogs already on the Internet by that time, and so I had no idea why anyone would possibly want to read anything that I had to say, but I decided to try it. I began with a few free Blogger blogs, and my readership in those days could have been measured with a magnifying glass.

But I stuck with it.

And that is one of the keys to success in any area of life. So many people give up if they don't have immediate success. And that is so sad, because all "overnight success stories" had to start somewhere.

So do not despise small beginnings - they can ultimately lead to something great.

Eventually my readership began to grow, and the real turning point for me came when I left the legal world at the end of 2009 and started *The Economic Collapse Blog*. Of course that had very humble beginnings as well. The first month the site was live I only had about 4,800 pageviews. But that was a whole lot more than I had before.

Very early on I decided that I was going to try to put out the highest quality articles that I could possibly write, and people really responded to that. They knew that they weren't getting straight answers about the economy from the mainstream media, and they were seeking out alternative sources of information. We have seen the "alternative media" absolutely explode in recent years, and I am proud to be part of that revolution.

In early 2010, my wife and I decided to take a leap and move across the country to a little town outside of Seattle, Washington. We didn't really have much money, so it was kind of a crazy thing to do. But we felt called to do it, so by faith we packed up our lives and moved all the way across the continent. We figured that I could make a little money writing and she could make a little money painting furniture and we could figure out a way to survive somehow.

We spent a little over a year out near Seattle, and during that time *The Economic Collapse Blog* started to grow by leaps and bounds. We also had other websites such as *End Of The American Dream* and *The Most Important News* that were really starting to grow as well, and so we felt secure enough to seek out a more permanent home. That was always the plan anyway, because we wanted to get away from the large population centers.

God eventually led us to a wonderful home in the mountains in a very isolated part of the northwest United States. And my wife and I both agree that this is the best place that either of us have ever lived. We absolutely love the peace and quiet, and the view that we have across the valley is priceless. I could have very easily sat up on that mountain living a very quiet life for the rest of my days and been very happy.

But God had other things in mind for us. When we moved up there, we believed that God was instructing us to prepare for what He wanted us to do. So we studied, and we prayed and we kept working on our websites. And then we studied, and we prayed and we worked some more. We never knew what kinds of doors God was going to open up for us. By faith we just tried to do what we believed that He was instructing us to do.

And of course many of you already know about the amazing doors that God has been opening up for us over the past few years. He is doing things that I never even would have imagined asking Him to do.

The reason why I am sharing all of this is to say that if someone like me can be used to make a difference, so can you.

If a completely anonymous Washington D.C. lawyer can move to the mountains in the middle of nowhere and be used to touch millions of lives all over the planet, that just shows that all things are possible with God.

Of course not everyone has a talent for writing. But we all have some way to make a difference. Individually, each one of us in limited, but collectively we can make a massive difference in this world if we are willing to work together.

When I was growing up, I wanted to be a rock star someday, but to this day I still don't have any musical talent. However, there are people out there with amazing gifts in that area, and I often find myself in awe of their talents.

Other people can make a difference in other areas. What some people are able to do with YouTube videos absolutely amazes me. Others write gripping novels or host amazing radio shows. And yet others organize street protests or get heavily involved in local politics.

We all have different gifts and abilities, and we all have ways that we can make a difference.

Part of my message is to warn people about the incredibly hard times that are coming, but part of my message is also to give hope to people so that they can come through those hard times successfully.

You may choose to curse the darkness when it comes, but I plan on lighting a candle.

No matter how bad things may get, I will not bend, I will not break and I will not fear. It is when times are the darkest that the greatest heroes are needed, and we need people that are going to be willing to face the great challenges that are coming with tremendous strength and courage.

Even in the midst of all of the chaos and all of the darkness, my wife and I believe that the greatest chapters of our lives are still ahead of us.

And we invite you to work with us to make a difference. God took the broken pieces of our lives and turned them into a beautiful thing, and He can do the same thing for you.

No matter how hard things may seem right now, please do not give up.

It's not over.

In fact, your future is only just beginning, and all things are possible...

-CHAPTER EIGHTEEN-

"It is the things that you do consistently that define who you are."

You are your habits. If you stop and think about this for a while, you will see that this is true. For example, if you go to the gym one time does that make you a bodybuilder? And if you go skiing one time does that make you a skier? The answers to those questions are obvious. If you want to be known for something, a certain amount of commitment is required. And you will find that those that never seem to amount to anything in life are often people that have trouble with commitment.

There are so many people that will get really excited about something but then never follow through. I have seen this over and over again throughout my life. Someone will get really excited about taking vitamins, but after a few days the excitement fades and the newly purchased bottles of vitamins sit in the cabinet collecting dust for months on end.

Will taking vitamins for a few days make any sort of a measurable difference in your health?

No, but taking them consistently as part of your normal daily routine sure will.

Or how often have we seen someone get pumped up for a diet for a little while only to return to their old eating patterns shortly thereafter?

Once in a while I get accused of being "predictable", but that is just because I do so many of the same things over and over again. My wife and I begin each day reading the Bible and praying, because doing those things develops spiritual maturity. And we take vitamins and superfood supplements with our meals because they provide the fuel that we need to be our best. I could go on and on, but I think that you get the point. Even in this book you will notice many of the same phrases coming up over and over, because they literally have become part of who I am. What we do and say and think consistently can literally change us down to the DNA level.

One of the ways that you can take control of your life is to take control of your habits. You want to develop habits that will help you to become the person that God created you to be.

And so how do we know what sorts of habits that we should be developing? Well, as I have explained elsewhere in this book, the Bible is God's instruction manual for life. If we incorporate the values and the principles that are laid out for us in the Word of God, good things will happen to us. If we choose to reject God's values and principles, that will only lead to pain, sorrow and heartbreak.

Earlier in this book, I talked about how loving God is one of the keys to living a life that really matters.

But how specifically do we love God?

Throughout the Scriptures, loving God and keeping His commandments are linked over and over again. The following are just a few examples...

John 14:15: *If ye love me, keep my commandments.*

John 14:21: *He that hath my commandments, and keepeth them, he it is that loveth me: and he that loveth me shall be loved of my Father, and I will love him, and will manifest myself to him.*

John 15:10: *If ye keep my commandments, ye shall abide in my love; even as I have kept my Father's commandments, and abide in his love.*

1 John 2:3: *And hereby we do know that we know him, if we keep his commandments.*

1 John 2:4: *He that saith, I know him, and keepeth not his commandments, is a liar, and the truth is not in him.*

1 John 3:24: *And he that keepeth his commandments dwelleth in him, and he in him. And hereby we know that he abideth in us, by the Spirit which he hath given us.*

1 John 5:2: *By this we know that we love the children of God, when we love God, and keep his commandments.*

In fact, the New Testament definition of "sin" is violation of God's commandments. We read the following in 1 John 3:4...

Whosoever committeth sin transgresseth also the law: for sin is the transgression of the law.

So if you want to start developing good habits, dig into the Word of God and find out what He wants you to do.

And once you discover those things, start doing them on a consistent basis.

It sounds so simple, but such a small percentage of the population is actually putting this into practice.

Instead, most people out there are enslaved to habits that they thought would make them happy but instead are only making them miserable.

One that I tend to bring up in my writing over and over again is pornography addiction. According to a survey conducted for Proven Men Ministries, 64 percent of all Christian men watch pornography "at least once a month". And according to Charisma News, another survey found that 68 percent of all Christian men watch pornography "on a regular basis".

Those numbers are absolutely shocking. It wasn't American men in general that were being asked about pornography use in those two surveys. Only "Christian men" were being surveyed, and if these numbers are accurate it would explain why the church in America today is so impotent.

If you are addicted to pornography, it will slowly destroy everything in your life. But of course the same could be said about drugs, alcohol, gambling and so many other self-destructive habits. The good news is that there is always a way out through Jesus Christ. If you repent and turn to Him, He will forgive all of your sins and will change you so that you eventually will not even want to engage in those extremely destructive behaviors any longer.

When you are extremely addicted to something, there are times when it can seem like it will be impossible to ever get free. That is why it can be so helpful to get involved in a support group where you can hear from others that are fighting the same battles.

If you try to break a bad addiction through your own power, there is a very high probability that you will fail, but if you lean on God you will find that all things are possible.

Have you noticed that I keep saying that a lot?

Repetition is the key to learning, and after you are done with this book some of the things that I have hammered on over and over will stick with you forever.

And there is no addiction that is so powerful that Jesus Christ cannot break it. He can take the broken pieces of your life and turn them into a beautiful thing, but the choice is up to you.

-CHAPTER NINETEEN-

"What you feed your mind will determine who you become."

How often have I written about the mainstream media? There are very powerful people that want to shape how we all think, and they are succeeding on a grand scale. I have shared the information in this chapter before, and I am sharing it again because it is absolutely imperative that people begin to understand these things. Breaking free from "the matrix" is one of the most important keys to living a life that really matters, and I hope that this chapter is a wake up call for many of you.

If you allow anyone to pump hours of "programming" into your mind every single day, it is inevitable that it is eventually going to have a major impact on how you view the world. In America today, the average person consumes approximately 10 hours of information, news and entertainment a day, and there are 6 giant media corporations that overwhelmingly dominate that market. In fact, it has been estimated that somewhere around 90 percent of the "programming" that we constantly feed our minds comes from them, and of course they are ultimately controlled by the elite of the world. So is there any hope for our country as long as the vast majority of the population is continually plugging themselves into this enormous "propaganda matrix"?

Just think about your own behavior. Even as you are reading this article the television might be playing in the background or you may have some music on. Many of us have gotten to the point where we are literally addicted to media. In fact, there are people out there that actually become physically uncomfortable if everything is turned off and they have to deal with complete silence.

It has been said that if you put garbage in, you are going to get garbage out. It is the things that we do consistently that define who we are, and so if you are feeding your mind with hours of "programming" from the big media corporations each day, that is going to have a dramatic effect on who you eventually become.

These monolithic corporations really do set the agenda for what society focuses on. For example, when you engage in conversation with your family, friends or co-workers, what do you talk about? If you are like most people, you might talk about something currently in the news, a television show that you watched last night or some major sporting event that is taking place.

Virtually all of that news and entertainment is controlled by the elite by virtue of their ownership of these giant media corporations.

I want to share some numbers with you that may be hard to believe. They come directly out of Nielsen's "Total Audience Report", and they show how much news and entertainment the average American consumes through various methods each day...

Watching live television: 4 hours, 32 minutes

Watching time-shifted television: 30 minutes

Listening to the radio: 2 hours, 44 minutes

Using a smartphone: 1 hour, 33 minutes

Using Internet on a computer: 1 hour, 6 minutes

When you add all of those numbers together, it comes to a grand total of more than 10 hours.

And keep in mind that going to movie theaters, playing video games and reading books are behaviors that are not even on this list.

What in the world are we doing to ourselves?

The combination of watching live television and watching time-shifted television alone comes to a total of more than five hours.

If you feed five hours of something into your mind day after day, **it is going to change you**. There is no way around that. You may think that you are strong enough to resist the programming, but the truth is that it affects all of us in very subtle ways that we do not even understand.

And as I mentioned above, there are just six giant corporations that account for almost all of the programming that we receive through our televisions. Below is a list of these six corporations along with a sampling of the various media properties that they own...

Comcast

NBC
Telemundo
Universal Pictures
Focus Features
USA Network
Bravo
CNBC
The Weather Channel
MSNBC
Syfy
NBCSN
Golf Channel
Esquire Network
E!
Cloo

Chiller
Universal HD
Comcast SportsNet
Universal Parks & Resorts
Universal Studio Home Video

The Walt Disney Company

ABC Television Network
ESPN
The Disney Channel
A&E
Lifetime
Marvel Entertainment
Lucasfilm
Walt Disney Pictures
Pixar Animation Studios
Disney Mobile
Disney Consumer Products
Interactive Media
Disney Theme Parks
Disney Records
Hollywood Records
Miramax Films
Touchstone Pictures

News Corporation

Fox Broadcasting Company
Fox News Channel
Fox Business Network
Fox Sports 1
Fox Sports 2
National Geographic
Nat Geo Wild
FX
FXX
FX Movie Channel
Fox Sports Networks

The Wall Street Journal
The New York Post
Barron's
SmartMoney
HarperCollins
20th Century Fox
Fox Searchlight Pictures
Blue Sky Studios
Beliefnet
Zondervan

Time Warner

CNN
The CW
HBO
Cinemax
Cartoon Network
HLN
NBA TV
TBS
TNT
TruTV
Turner Classic Movies
Warner Bros.
Castle Rock
DC Comics
Warner Bros. Interactive Entertainment
New Line Cinema
Sports Illustrated
Fortune
Marie Claire
People Magazine

Viacom

MTV
Nickelodeon
VH1

BET
Comedy Central
Paramount Pictures
Paramount Home Entertainment
Country Music Television (CMT)
Spike TV
The Movie Channel
TV Land

CBS Corporation

CBS Television Network
The CW (along with Time Warner)
CBS Sports Network
Showtime
TVGN
CBS Radio, Inc.
CBS Television Studios
Simon & Schuster
Infinity Broadcasting
Westwood One Radio Network

Fortunately, those enormous media conglomerates do not have quite the same power over the Internet, but we are starting to see a tremendous amount of consolidation in the online world as well. At this point, the top 10 publishers account for nearly half of all traffic to news websites. The alternative media is definitely growing, but it is very tough to compete with that kind of power.

The battle for the future of this nation is a battle for the hearts and minds of individuals.

And it is hard to see how things will be turned in a dramatically different direction as long as most of us are willingly feeding our hearts and minds with hours of "programming" that is controlled by the elite each day.

The good news is that there are signs of an awakening. More Americans than ever are becoming disenchanted with the mainstream media, and this is showing up in recent survey numbers. For example, one recent survey found that only 6 percent of Americans "have a lot of confidence in the media" at this point.

As Americans (and people all over the world) have lost confidence in the mainstream media, they have been seeking out other sources of news and entertainment. You can only enslave people for so long. Ultimately, they will want to break free of the chains that are holding them back and they will want to find the truth.

In this day and age, it is absolutely imperative that we all learn to think for ourselves. If you find that you are still addicted to the "programming" that the giant media corporations are feeding you, I would encourage you to start unplugging from the matrix more frequently.

In the end, you will be glad that you did.

CHAPTER TWENTY

"Life without fear."

This is a really good time for me to write this chapter, because many of the things that I am going to share I need to be reminded of myself. Just yesterday, I received some very troubling news. I found out that someone that I respect had done something that threatened to totally derail a project that I had already invested a tremendous amount of time and energy into. Almost immediately after I got this news, the enemy started to try to hit me with doubt, worry, anxiety and fear.

But that isn't how my wife and I live our lives, and so the enemy was not successful. In 1 John 4:18 we are told that "perfect love casteth out fear", and because of God's radical love for us we are able to live lives that are free of doubt, worry, anxiety and fear. Even though our lives are crazy and the world around us is becoming more unstable with each passing day, we aren't on any medications and we sleep very peacefully at night.

My wife and I seek to live in a constant state of "shalom", which many of you probably already know is the Hebrew word for peace. But it actually goes much deeper than that. According to Wikipedia, shalom "is a Hebrew word meaning peace, harmony, wholeness, completeness, prosperity, welfare and tranquility". It also carries with it a sense of balance.

When we live in "shalom", our lives are not governed by the ups and downs of daily life. We know who we belong to, what our mission is, and where we are ultimately going. No matter what anyone else does or says, it is not going to tip us out of balance because our lives have a solid foundation.

So getting back to the project that I am working on, I decided to go ahead with it anyway because in the end it is God that is in control. As long as I am in the center of His will, nothing is going to derail the purposes and the plans that He has for me.

But I didn't always have this perspective on life. Growing up, I was like most Americans. I was constantly consumed by doubt, worry, anxiety and fear. And actually worry, anxiety and fear are all very, very closely related. When you don't trust that God has control of your future, it can be very easy to view the future negatively.

Today, most people would not admit to being "fearful", but there certainly is a lot of "worry" and "anxiety" going around. In fact, according to the Anxiety and Depression Association of America anxiety disorders "cost the U.S. more than $42 billion a year, almost one-third of the country's $148 billion total mental health bill".

But Jesus offers us a better way. He taught us that we are not to be anxious about anything in our lives. The following is what Luke 12:22-31 says in the Modern English Version...

22 Then He said to His disciples, "Therefore I say to you, do not be anxious for your life, what you will eat, nor for your body, what you will wear. 23 Life is more than food, and the body is more than clothes. 24 Consider the ravens: They neither sow nor reap, they have neither storehouses nor barns. Yet God feeds them. How much more valuable are you than birds? 25 Who of you by worrying can add one cubit to his height? 26 If you then cannot do what is least, why are you anxious about the other things?

27 "Consider how the lilies grow. They neither spin nor weave. Yet I say to you that Solomon in all his glory was not arrayed like one of these. 28 If God so clothes the grass, which today is in the field and tomorrow is thrown into the oven, how much more will He clothe you, O you of little faith? 29 And do not seek what you will eat or what you will drink, nor be of an anxious mind. 30 For the nations of the world seek all these things, and your Father knows that you need them. 31 But seek the kingdom of God, and all these things shall be given to you.

It is easy to say that we should seek God's kingdom first, but it is another thing entirely to put that into practice.

If you are anything like me, there are constantly things that are trying to tear your attention away from the things that really matter, and it takes a lot of determination to keep your focus where it should be.

But if we can keep our eyes fixed on Jesus, everything else just seems to fall into place.

If you ever start to feel worry, anxiety or fear starting to creep back in, just start to pray. I really like how Philippians 4:6-8 is rendered in the Modern English Version...

6 Be anxious for nothing, but in everything, by prayer and supplication with gratitude, make your requests known to God. 7 And the peace of God, which surpasses all understanding, will protect your hearts and minds through Christ Jesus.

In those verses we are told that instead of being anxious about something, we should take it to prayer instead. When we choose to dwell on anxious thoughts, that is a response that comes from a lack of faith. But when we pray, that shows that we have enough faith to trust God with an answer to our problem.

And sometimes it is going to take an extended period of prayer before we feel peace. It can be tempting to give up after just a few minutes if it doesn't feel like it is "working", but it is those that persist that end up getting their breakthroughs.

There are so many out there that don't understand that prayer involves two way communication. Sometimes when we are firing off our lists of all the things that we want to change, He is trying to get us to understand that we are the ones that actually need to change.

And there is nothing that will change you faster than being in the presence of God. When you truly open up your heart and being to praise and worship Him, you will find that worry, anxiety and fear will quickly melt away.

Yes, there will always be challenges in life. But when you surrender everything to Him, it truly does become possible to live a life that is completely without fear.

-CHAPTER TWENTY ONE-

"Why Complain When You Can Be Grateful Instead?"

Have you ever been around someone that is a chronic complainer? It isn't a pleasant experience. For the chronic complainer, nothing is ever good enough. No matter how good things are going, and no matter how much others have done for them, chronic complainers will always find something to complain about.

I don't know about you, but I go out of my way to stay away from people that want to constantly complain about everything. They just seem to suck all of the joy out of a room, and I find that most people tend to gravitate away from those that grumble and complain all the time. But it is really easy to point a finger at others that are complaining and yet so easy to slip into such a pattern ourselves.

When things aren't going well, instead of focusing on solutions often our first instinct is to start complaining. But complaining never actually accomplishes much of anything. All that it usually does is annoy everyone around us.

Many of us mastered the art of complaining as teenagers. No matter how good our parents were to us, we always had to act unimpressed and had to find something to complain about. Many teens may think that this makes them look "grown up", but instead it just makes them very unpleasant to be around. Looking back now, I wish that I would have had a much different attitude as a teen.

And so many of the same principles apply to our relationship with God. Even though He has given us His very best by sending His Son to die on the cross for us, many of us tend to want to complain to Him about just about everything in our lives. During our prayer times, we will rattle off very long lists of what we want done, and then when He does come through for us in incredible ways many of us will completely forget to thank Him. I will address this more in a moment.

Just like us, God is not a big fan of grumblers and complainers. In the Torah, over and over again we see the people of Israel complaining, and over and over again God judges them for it. In Numbers 14:26-31, we find one of the more prominent examples of this...

26 The Lord spoke to Moses and to Aaron, saying: 27 How long will this evil assembly be murmuring against Me? I have heard the murmurings of the children of Israel which they murmur against Me. 28 Say to them, "As I live," says the Lord, "just as you have spoken in My ears, so I will do to you. 29 In this wilderness your corpses will fall, and all who were numbered of you, according to your whole number, from twenty years old and upward, who have murmured against Me, 30 you will not go into the land which I swore by My hand to cause you to dwell in it, except Caleb the son of Jephunneh and Joshua the son of Nun. 31 But your children, whom you said would be a prey, I will bring them in and they will know the land, which you rejected.

God was ready to take that generation into the promised land, but they refused to believe that He would enable them to defeat the evil nations that were already living there. And as the Lord took them toward the promised land, they were constantly grumbling and complaining about various things even though they had just seen all of the incredible miracles that the Lord had performed in bringing them out of the land of Egypt.

So even though God had wanted to take that generation into the promised land, they missed out on their breakthrough because of their horrible attitudes.

And if we are not careful, we can miss out on so much in life as well if our attitudes are bad.

God has a unique path for each one of our lives, and those paths are not always going to be easy. But the Lord wants us to learn how to be content in any situation. We need to have the same kind of perspective that the Apostle Paul did. The following is how Philippians 4:11-13 reads in the Modern English Version...

11 I do not speak because I have need, for I have learned in whatever state I am to be content. 12 I know both how to face humble circumstances and how to have abundance. Everywhere and in all things I have learned the secret, both to be full and to be hungry, both to abound and to suffer need. 13 I can do all things because of Christ who strengthens me.

But in addition to being content in every circumstance, we need to strive to be grateful.

Have you ever gone out of your way to do something really nice for someone and then not get thanked at all for doing it?

How did you feel about that person afterwards?

Being grateful shows humility, and it also shows that you care about the time, effort and energy that someone else has expended on your behalf.

If we choose not to be grateful, it is unlikely that others will want to help us again in the future. So it is actually in your best interest to cultivate a thankful attitude, but even more importantly 1 Thessalonians 5:18 tells us that being thankful is God's will for us...

In every thing give thanks: for this is the will of God in Christ Jesus concerning you.

And life is just so much sweeter when you decide that you want to live life with gratefulness.

If you are a chronic complainer, just try it some time. Instead of starting your day by complaining about how miserable everything is, try thinking of things that you are thankful for.

And if you are having a tough time with this, just start with things that are really basic.

We can all be thankful that we have been given another day to be alive.

We can all be thankful for the people that love us and care for us.

We can all be thankful that we have food to eat and a warm place to sleep.

And above everything else, if we know the Lord Jesus Christ we can be thankful that our sins are forgiven and that we have been given eternal life. If you do not know the Lord Jesus Christ yet, there is an entire chapter at the end of this book entitled "The Most Important Thing" that explains in detail how you can.

If you are not accustomed to being grateful, it can take a bit of practice at first, but if you stick with it you will soon discover that your entire approach to life has changed.

Life is good, and God has given us so much to be thankful for.

We just need to open up our eyes and see it.

-CHAPTER TWENTY TWO-

"Always Have Something For A Rainy Day."

No matter how well you plan, someday something is going to go wrong. As the publisher of *The Economic Collapse Blog*, people often write to me and ask me financial questions, and the number one thing that I always suggest to people is to have an emergency fund.

Most of this chapter is based on an article that I recently published, but I wanted to include it here because it is so critically important. If you don't have anything to fall back on, you and your family could suddenly lose everything in the event of a significant tragedy such as a job loss or a death in the family.

Do you have an emergency fund? If you even have one penny in emergency savings, you are already ahead of about one-fourth of the country. I write about this stuff all the time, but it always astounds me how many Americans are literally living on the edge financially. Back in 2008 when the economy tanked and millions of people lost their jobs, large numbers of Americans suddenly couldn't pay their bills because they were living paycheck to paycheck. Now the stage is set for it to happen again. Another major recession is going to happen at some point, and when it does millions of people are going to get blindsided by it.

Despite all of our emphasis on education, we never seem to teach our young people how to handle money. But this is one of the most basic skills that everyone needs. Personally, I went through high school, college and law school without ever being taught about the dangers of going into debt or the importance of saving money.

If you are ever going to build any wealth, you have got to spend less than you earn. That is just basic common sense.

Unfortunately, nearly one out of every four Americans does not have even a single penny in emergency savings...

Bankrate's newly released June Financial Security Index survey indicates that 24 percent of Americans have not saved any money at all for their emergency funds.

This is despite experts recommending that people strive for a savings cushion equivalent to the amount needed to cover three to six months' worth of expenses.

(http://www.dailymail.co.uk/news/article-4622700/24-percent-Americans-ZERO-savings-emergencies.html)

For years, I have been telling my readers that at a minimum they need to have an emergency fund that can cover at least six months of expenses. It is great to have more than that, but everyone should strive to have at least a six month cushion.

Unfortunately, that same Bankrate survey found that only 31 percent of Americans actually have such a cushion...

The June survey also found that 31 percent of Americans have what Bankrate considers an 'adequate' savings cushion — six or more months' worth of money to pay expenses — which means that nearly two-thirds of the country isn't saving enough money.

(http://www.dailymail.co.uk/news/article-4622700/24-percent-Americans-ZERO-savings-emergencies.html)

That means that a whopping 69 percent of all Americans do not have an adequate emergency fund.

So what is going to happen if another great crisis arrives and millions of people suddenly lose their jobs?

Just like last time, mortgage defaults will start soaring and countless numbers of families will lose their homes.

If you do not have anything to fall back on, you can lose your spot in the middle class really fast. And in the case of a truly catastrophic national crisis, trying to operate without any money at all is going to be exceedingly challenging.

Just recently, the Federal Reserve conducted a survey that discovered that 44 percent of all Americans do not even have enough money "to cover an unexpected $400 expense".

That is almost half the country.

And a different survey by CareerBuilder found that 75 percent of all Americans have lived paycheck to paycheck "at least some of the time".

Unfortunately, in a desperate attempt to make ends meet many of us continue to pile up more and more debt. According to Moneyish, Americans have now accumulated more than a trillion dollars of credit card debt, more than a trillion dollars of student loan debt, and more than a trillion dollars of auto loan debt...

We've racked up $1 trillion in credit card debt — and that's just a fraction of what we owe. That's according to data released this year from the Federal Reserve, which found that U.S. consumers owe $1.0004 trillion on their cards, up 6.2% from a year ago; this is the highest amount owed since January 2009. What's more, this isn't the only consumer debt to top $1 trillion. We now also owe more than $1 trillion for our cars, and for our student loans, the data showed.

(https://moneyish.com/ish/5-facts-that-prove-americans-dont-know-anything-about-managing-money/)

Overall, U.S. consumers are now more than 12 trillion dollars in debt.

We often criticize the federal government for being nearly 20 trillion dollars in debt, and that criticism is definitely valid. What we are doing to future generations of Americans is beyond criminal and it needs to stop.

But are we not doing something similar to ourselves?

When you divide the total amount of consumer debt by the size of the U.S. population, it breaks down to roughly $40,000 for every man, woman and child in our country.

When someone lends you money, you have to pay back more than you originally borrow. And in the case of high interest debt, you can end up paying back several times what you originally borrowed.

If you carry a balance from month to month on a high interest credit card, it is absolutely crippling you financially. But many Americans don't understand this. Instead, they just keep sending off the "minimum payment" every month because that is the easiest thing to do.

If you ever want to achieve financial freedom, you have got to get rid of your toxic debts. There are some forms of low interest debt, such as mortgage debt, that are not going to financially cripple you. But anything with a high rate of interest you will want to pay off as soon as possible.

And everyone needs a financial cushion. Unless you can guarantee that your life is always going to go super smoothly and that you are never going to have any problems, you need an emergency fund to fall back on.

Yes, you may need to make some sacrifices in order to make that happen. Nobody ever said that it would be easy. But just about everyone has somewhere that a little "belt tightening" can be done, and in the long-term it will be worth it.

When you don't have to constantly worry about how you are going to pay the bills next month, it will help you sleep a lot easier at night. Many of us have put a lot of unnecessary stress on ourselves by spending money that we didn't have for things that we really didn't need.

And now is the time to get your financial house in order, because it appears that another major economic downturn is not too far away.

-CHAPTER TWENTY THREE-

"Don't Give In To The Hate."

What do you think would happen to our society if we decided to just start loving one another? I am writing this at a time when the United States is the most polarized that it has been in decades. Democrats hate Republicans and Republicans hate Democrats, but all of this hate is not really getting us anywhere. I think that most of us have forgotten that we are supposed to love our enemies. If we only love those that agree with us and that are just like us, what is that going to accomplish?

Following the election in November, there were news reports about leftists that were being "triggered" simply by seeing the name of Trump somewhere. I don't know if I have ever seen so much rage directed at a new president, and some of the things that are being said and done by those on the left are absolutely frightening.

For instance, Kathy Griffin made national headlines when she posed for photographs "with a 'beheaded' President Trump"...

Kathy Griffin sent shockwaves through the internet when she posed with a "beheaded" President Trump.

The comedian looks somber in pictures that are reminiscent of ISIS beheading videos and photos. She holds a facsimile of Mr. Trump's detached, bloodied head by the hair.

The photo was taken by Tyler Shields, who is known for controversial art, including a photo of Clint Eastwood's daughter burning a $100,000 Hermes handbag.

(http://www.cbsnews.com/news/kathy-griffin-takes-photos-with-beheaded-trump/)

Why would someone do such a thing?

Following that, there was a huge controversy surrounding a New York theater group which produced a twisted version of "Julius Caesar" in which a character that is dressed up just like Donald Trump is viciously assassinated at the end of the play. The following comes from Piers Morgan...

The play portrays Caesar as a tempestuous, petulant blond-haired businessman in an expensive business suit with an American pin flag and over-long ties who takes baths in a gold bathtub.

His wife Calpurnia has an Eastern European accent and wears designer clothes.

So, it's Donald Trump.

It ends with Caesar/Trump being brutally murdered by Roman senators who fear he has become too power hungry.

Only in this case, the assassins are all women and minorities, two groups that Trump has been accused of marginalising.

(http://www.dailymail.co.uk/news/article-4596300/PIERS-MORGAN-Hate-filled-liberals-bad-Trump-death-jokes.html)

By the end of the assassination scene, Trump's shirt is absolutely soaked with blood, and it is quite obvious that the producers intended to create a spectacle that is as gruesome as they could possibly get away with.

But instead of reacting to this play with horror, many on the left are absolutely gushing over it. For instance, CNN's Fareed Zakaria actually called it "a masterpiece".

And of course worst of all was when 66-year-old James Hodgkinson attempted to gun down as many Republican members of Congress as possible at a baseball field in Virginia. It turns out that he was a huge fan of Bernie Sanders and Rachel Maddow, and after listening to so much hate day after day he eventually just snapped.

Many of those on the left have no idea why they are feeling so much rage. They just know that Trump is on the "wrong team" and that he supposedly stands for things that they aren't supposed to like. But if you would ask many of them to put their feelings into words, most of them would not be able to do so in a cohesive manner.

Of course many on the right have heaped a tremendous amount of abuse on Barack Obama and Hillary Clinton in recent years. Even though they stand for things that are truly appalling, does that justify the horrible mistreatment that they have received?

You can love people without agreeing with them. In fact, you can deeply love someone and still disapprove of every single thing that they stand for. And even though Barack Obama and Hillary Clinton are both completely unfit to hold any political office anywhere in the country, that doesn't mean that we should hate them. Like so many other political leaders, Obama and Clinton have done some exceedingly terrible things, but that doesn't mean that they are beyond all hope. All of us have done things that we are now ashamed of, and all of us have needed some grace at various points in our lives. We should always be willing to love our political enemies, to forgive them, to pray for them, and we should always want the very best for them and for their families.

As it stands, America is at a very dangerous place because of all of the anger and frustration that are boiling just under the surface. According to a recent Reuters survey, only 25 percent of Americans believe that the country is heading in the right direction, and the protests in our streets have turned increasingly violent in recent years.

Many on the left are using terms such as "Nazi", "racist" and "dictator" to describe Donald Trump, and that is the kind of language that can spur people to take violent action. There are some that believe that America is heading for a "civil war", and there are others that believe that one has already started. But none of us should ever want that to actually happen.

In my adult life, I have never seen America so divided, but it doesn't have to be this way.

What if we decided to start loving one another no matter what we look like, where we are from or who our ancestors were?

What if we decided to start loving one another no matter who we voted for or what our particular political beliefs may be?

What if we decided to start loving one another no matter how much the mainstream media, our politicians and the entertainment community tried to stir up hate?

Not too long ago, a distant relative decided to cut off all communication with Meranda and I simply because of a pro-Trump article that I authored. Apparently someone must be anti-Trump in order to be loved and accepted by this particular individual.

Of course similar things are happening all over the country because of animosity toward Trump.

But if we are not willing to talk with one another, how will we ever solve any of the problems that this nation is facing?

Don't get me wrong. I am certainly not suggesting that we should ever compromise our most cherished values and principles. If the left is going to hate us because we refuse to move from the values and the principles that this nation was founded upon, there isn't much we can do about that.

But even though they may hate us, we can choose to love them. When we do good to those that hate us, it has a far more powerful effect than if we return hate with more hate. The following is one of the most famous quotes from Dr. Martin Luther King Jr...

Darkness cannot drive out darkness;
only light can do that.
Hate cannot drive out hate;
only love can do that.
Hate multiplies hate,
violence multiplies violence,
and toughness multiplies toughness
in a descending spiral of destruction....
The chain reaction of evil --
hate begetting hate,
wars producing more wars --
must be broken,
or we shall be plunged
into the dark abyss of annihilation.

Those are very wise words.

We will never defeat the leftists that are trying to destroy our nation by hating them. But if we shower them with light and love many of them will eventually come over to our side.

I am a big believer in the marketplace of ideas, because I also believe that truth always wins in the end. If we can respectfully engage with those that disagree with us and show them that there is a better way, we will win many of them over.

One of the reasons why the left has made so much progress in recent decades is because most of the population has abandoned the core values that once made America so great. If we rediscover those values, they can provide a basis for healing and reuniting our broken nation.

For example, in the Declaration of Independence our forefathers declared that "all men are created equal". We should all be able to agree that every single individual is of immense value, and that all of us should be treated equally under the law no matter where we came from, no matter what our skin color is and no matter how much money we have.

The Declaration of Independence also tells us that we have been endowed "with certain unalienable Rights, that among these are Life, Liberty and the pursuit of Happiness". If you follow my work on a regular basis, you know that first one is absolutely huge for me. Elsewhere in this book I am going to spend an entire chapter on that topic. But for the moment I want to focus on Liberty. In every human heart there is a desire to live free. This is one of the reasons why big government liberalism is such a bankrupt philosophy. Big government always ends in tyranny, and I don't know any true American that actually wants tyranny.

There are so many things that both the left and the right should be able to agree upon.

One is that Congress has become a cesspool of filth and corruption. Can't we agree that the way that we run our elections needs to be greatly reformed and that special interests and big donors should have much less influence in Washington D.C.?

Another thing that we should be able to agree upon is that we should have a country where freedom and liberty are maximized. Instinctively, most of us want to live our lives without someone else constantly telling us what to do. We all proudly sing that we are "the land of the free", and we need to start making that a reality once again.

We should also all be able to agree that terrorism is a growing problem, and that we should do all that we can to keep our communities safe. Of course there are disagreements about how precisely to do that, but in the face of a common enemy that is intent on destroying us the American people should be able to come together.

In addition, we should all be able to agree that we need to strengthen the Social Security system so that it will always be there for retiring Americans that need it. Unfortunately, our politicians raided the Social Security trust fund and have badly mismanaged the system, and so now the future of the program looks shaky. But we should be able to work together to get it back on solid ground once again.

Of course all of us want an economy that is vibrant and growing, and that hasn't been true for a very long time. Barack Obama was the only president in U.S. history not to have a single year when the economy grew by at least three percent, and over the past ten years U.S. GDP growth has averaged just 1.33 percent per year. If we would just take the shackles off of the economy we could do so much better. The greatest era of economic growth in our history was when there was no Federal Reserve, no IRS and no income tax, and we can do it again.

We all want better lives for our families and our communities, and we can make America great again if we start doing the things that made America great in the first place.

Ultimately, much of this book is about restoring American values. It is about restoring God, family and country to their proper places and getting our priorities back in order. It is about learning to love others the way that we love ourselves.

It has been said that a house divided against itself will surely fall. And if we continue down this road of hatred and division, America will surely fall no matter what ideology eventually triumphs.

There is nothing that says that we all have to hate one another. It doesn't have to be this way, and we need a new generation of leaders that are willing to take us in a different direction.

Because right now what we are getting from the corporate media and most of our politicians is a steady stream of strife, discord, bitterness, resentment and hatred.

The only way that we are going to become "a shining city upon a hill" again is if we learn to love one another truly and deeply and from the heart. To close this chapter, let me share with you what President Ronald Reagan said about this shining city during his farewell address to the American people...

The past few days when I've been at that window upstairs, I've thought a bit of the "shining city upon a hill." The phrase comes from John Winthrop, who wrote it to describe the America he imagined. What he imagined was important because he was an early Pilgrim, an early freedom man. He journeyed here on what today we'd call a little wooden boat; and like the other Pilgrims, he was looking for a home that would be free.

I've spoken of the shining city all my political life, but I don't know if I ever quite communicated what I saw when I said it. But in my mind it was a tall, proud city built on rocks stronger than oceans, windswept, God-blessed, and teeming with people of all kinds living in harmony and peace; a city with free ports that hummed with commerce and creativity. And if there had to be city walls, the walls had doors and the doors were open to anyone with the will and the heart to get here. That's how I saw it, and see it still.

Reagan's dream is still alive, but in order to live in harmony and peace we must reject hatred and division.

Just because America is deeply divided today does not mean that all hope is lost.

There is a better way, and we can get there.

-CHAPTER TWENTY FOUR-

The Conclusion Of The Matter

I know that we have covered an enormous amount of material very rapidly in this book. Without a doubt, many of the chapters could have been expanded into an entire book themselves. But I wanted to pack as many secrets to living a life that really matters as I possibly could into this collection.

I truly believe that most of us have an inherent desire to live a life that is meaningful. Unfortunately, most of us have never been taught how to go about doing that. In school we were taught all sorts of facts and figures, but very little attention was ever paid to the big "why" questions.

As I conclude this book, I would like to take a look at King Solomon for a few moments. The Bible tells us that God gave Solomon extraordinary wisdom. For example, we read the following in 1 Kings 10...

23 So king Solomon exceeded all the kings of the earth for riches and for wisdom.

24 And all the earth sought to Solomon, to hear his wisdom, which God had put in his heart.

And in 1 Kings 4:32 we are told that Solomon produced three thousand proverbs and more than a thousand songs. Of course he also wrote most of the Book of Proverbs, the entire book of Song of Solomon and the entire Book of Ecclesiastes.

In the Book of Ecclesiastes, Solomon kind of looks back on his entire life and discusses many of the lessons that he has learned over that time. When we get to the very end of the book, he summarizes everything in one very simple conclusion. This is what Ecclesiastes 12:13-14 says...

13 Let us hear the conclusion of the whole matter: Fear God, and keep his commandments: for this is the whole duty of man.

14 For God shall bring every work into judgment, with every secret thing, whether it be good, or whether it be evil.

Once again, "fearing God" is not about being afraid of Him. Rather, we are to reverence, honor and respect Him. After everything that Solomon had been through, and after everything that he had learned throughout his lifetime, this is what he wanted to leave us with.

And ultimately this brings us full circle in this book. I started by discussing what Jesus taught about the greatest commandment. In Luke 10:27 Jesus instructs us to "love the Lord thy God with all thy heart, and with all thy soul, and with all thy strength, and with all thy mind; and thy neighbour as thyself".

In the end, it really is all about loving God and loving one another.

But it is one thing to intellectually know this, and it is another thing entirely to put it into practice.

The only way that you are going to be able to live a life of great love is to allow God's love to flow through you. And the only way that will be possible is if you have a personal relationship with Jesus Christ. The very last chapter in this book is entitled "The Most Important Thing", and if you currently do not have a personal relationship with Jesus Christ that chapter will explain how you can have one.

Whatever you are going through in life, the answer is Jesus.

I know that sounds incredibly simple, but it is true. No matter how bad things may seem right now, and no matter how messed up your life has become, Jesus can always turn things around. He loves you with a love that cannot be measured, and He is always just a prayer away.

The same principles apply on a national level.

The only answer to the problems that America is facing today is Jesus Christ. No matter how bad things have gotten, if we repent and start doing things the way that Jesus told us to do them we will be able to turn this country around.

Many on the left today want to drive God out of every corner of public life. That is the exact opposite of what we should be doing.

America was born out of culture that was Christian. According to Dr. Mark David Hall, 98 percent of the colonists in early America were Protestant, and another 1.9 percent were Roman Catholic. The laws of the original 13 colonies were very strongly based on the Bible, and sometimes entire blocks of text were pulled directly out of the Scriptures and incorporated into their statutes.

No book was quoted by our founders more than the Bible, and no book influenced them more than the Bible did. And one place we see this influence is in the famous words right at the beginning of the Declaration of Independence...

We hold these truths to be self-evident, that all men are created equal, that they are endowed by their Creator with certain unalienable Rights, that among these are Life, Liberty and the pursuit of Happiness.

But we don't want our politicians to talk like this today. Instead, most of us seem to think that we can make America great again without God.

That is simply not going to happen.

If we want to make America great again, we need to return to God and start keeping his commandments again.

To illustrate this, I would like to share with you an edited version of an article that I recently published about an extraordinary event that happened during Donald Trump's inauguration...

It was one of those magical moments that you will never forget. The inauguration of Donald Trump was being watched live by tens of millions of people all over the world, and it was at that precise moment that God gave all of us another little reminder that He is in control. It had not been raining prior to the time that Trump stepped up to the Inauguration platform, but when he did, the rain began to fall. Considering everything else that was going on at the time, it would have been really easy to miss that little detail, but fortunately there was someone there that perfectly understood what was happening.

When Rev. Franklin Graham came to the platform later on to deliver his portion of the benediction, it was perhaps the most electrifying moment of the entire event. Before reading the passage of Scripture that he had chosen, this is what Rev. Graham told the crowd...

"Mr. President, in the Bible, rain is a sign of God's blessing. And it started to rain, Mr. President, when you came to the platform. It's my prayer that God will bless you, your family, your administration, and may He bless America."

And Graham was exactly correct about this. All throughout the Bible, rain is an indication of the blessing of God. For example, in Leviticus 26:3-10 the people of Israel were told that rain would be one of the primary blessings that they would receive if they kept God's commandments...

3 If you walk in My statutes and keep My commandments and do them, 4 then I will give you rain in due season, and the land shall yield its increase, and the trees of the field shall yield their fruit. 5 Your threshing shall last till the grape harvest, and the grape harvest shall last till the time for sowing, and you shall eat your bread till you are full and dwell in your land safely.

6 I will give peace in the land, and you shall lie down for sleep, and none shall make you afraid; I will remove harmful beasts from the land, and the sword shall not go through your land. 7 You shall chase your enemies, and they shall fall before you by the sword. 8 Five of you shall chase a hundred, and a hundred of you shall put ten thousand to flight, and your enemies shall fall before you by the sword.

9 I will turn toward you and make you fruitful and multiply you, and I will confirm My covenant with you. 10 You shall eat the old harvest long stored, and clear out the old to make way for the new.

Alternatively, in Deuteronomy 11:16-17 the people of Israel were warned that if they turned away from the one true God and worshipped other gods that the Lord would withhold rain from them...

16 Take heed to yourselves that your heart be not deceived, and you turn away and serve other gods and worship them. 17 Then the Lord's wrath will be inflamed against you, and He will shut up the heavens so that there will be no rain and the land will not yield its fruit, and you will quickly perish from the good land which the Lord is giving you.

Now that he is the president, Donald Trump will have some very hard choices to make. Let us hope that he follows the one true God that created all things and makes decisions that are in line with His commandments and His statutes.

The Bible is very clear – if we love the one true God and keep His commandments, we will be blessed. As a nation, that is the path that we should take.

When Vice-President Mike Pence was sworn in, he had his hand on the same Bible and on the same Bible verse that Ronald Reagan did when he was inaugurated.

That verse was 2 Chronicles 7:14, and the verse immediately before that one talks about God withholding rain because of the wickedness of the people. Is that an absolutely amazing "coincidence" or what? This is what 2 Chronicles 7:13-14 says in the Modern English Version…

*13 "When I shut up the heaven and there is **no rain**, or when I command the locusts to devour the land, or send pestilence on My people, 14 if My people, who are called by My name, will humble themselves and pray, and seek My face and turn from their wicked ways, then I will hear from heaven, and will forgive their sin and will heal their land.*

Right after Pence was sworn in with his hand on these verses, Donald Trump stepped on to the platform to be inaugurated and the rain started to fall.

Could it be possible that God has given us this prophetic sign to show us that He is ready to forgive our national sins and heal our land if we will just turn to Him?

Many have pointed out that on Trump's first full day as president, he was 70 years, 7 months and 7 days old.

Is that just another "coincidence"?

And we just happen to be in year 5777 on the Hebrew calendar.

I believe that Donald Trump has some very important things that he is supposed to do, but of course the enemy will constantly be trying to steal that destiny from him.

And Donald Trump is going to be facing an internal battle as well. Washington D.C. has a way of changing people, and there will be constant pressure to turn from the straight and narrow path.

So let us pray for him and for all of our leaders, and let us also pray that our entire country will turn back to God so that a season of restoration can begin.

God is always trying to get our attention, but are we willing to listen?

Despite everything that has happened, God is still showing us grace and mercy. He wants us to repent and turn back to Him, but if we continue to push Him away eventually the time for grace and mercy will end.

We cannot continue to embrace just about every type of sin imaginable and expect that there will never be any consequences for our actions.

If we will turn back to God, the future of this nation could be greater than we could possibly imagine right now. But if we continue on the path that we are currently on, there won't be any future for this nation at all.

My hope is that America will wake up soon, because we are quickly running out of time.

-CHAPTER TWENTY FIVE-

A Personal Note: I Have Decided To Run For Congress

If you want to live a life that really matters, you have to be willing to take risks. The old phrase "nothing ventured, nothing gained" is so true. If you always play it safe you might very well make it a long way in life, but it is unlikely that you will ever accomplish anything truly great. God is looking for people that are ready to boldly step out in faith, and those that do often find that God does more for them than they ever dared to dream or imagine.

If you are familiar with my work, then you probably already know that I am running for Congress in the 1st congressional district here in Idaho. I hope to do another book soon that is focused on specific proposals for turning America around, but I knew that I couldn't ignore politics entirely in this one. So below I have briefly outlined where I stand on some of the most important issues of our day. If you happen to live in Idaho's 1st congressional district, I hope that you will prayerfully consider voting for me after reviewing my positions...

Faith: I am a Bible-believing Christian, and my faith provides a foundation for everything that I do and everything that I am. This nation was founded by Bible-believing Christians, and the Declaration of Independence and the U.S. Constitution were birthed out of the values and principles found in the Word of God. If we truly want to make America great again, we need to return to those values and principles.

Getting The Federal Government Off Of Our Backs: The balance of power between the federal government and the state governments needs to change dramatically. Here in Idaho, for way too long the control freaks in the federal government have been meddling in our affairs, and we need that to end. We need to get the federal government off of the backs of our farmers, our miners, our loggers and our ranchers. We need to end the federal mandates that are so costly for our state government, and we need to transfer control of federal lands to the people of Idaho. And we definitely don't want the federal government to resettle refugees from the Middle East into our communities without our consent.

Congress: If there is one institution that embodies the corruption that permeates Washington D.C., it is the United States Congress. Dominated by extremely selfish career politicians that are primarily interested in raising enough money to win their next elections, Congress has become a cesspool of filth, fraud and malfeasance. The American people are absolutely sick of this, and that is why approval ratings for Congress are consistently much lower than for any other political institution. Donald Trump captured the imagination of tens of millions of American voters when he pledged to "drain the swamp" during the last election, but I say that it is time to "flush the toilet" because the only way that we will ever be able to turn the federal government in a positive direction is if we clean out the halls of power in Washington.

Limited Government: Our founders intended to create a central government with very limited powers, but instead it has evolved into an absolute monster. We need to tame that monster and restore the constitutional balance of power that our founders originally intended.

Planned Parenthood: If I am elected, I will use the full power of my office to go to war with Planned Parenthood. Every single day, horrifying crimes against humanity are being committed at Planned Parenthood clinics all over the nation. Undercover investigations have revealed that body parts are being harvested from dead babies and sold off to the highest bidder, and this must be stopped immediately. I will be Planned Parenthood's number one enemy in

Congress, and I will never vote for any bill that grants them even a single penny of federal funding. Like many Pro-Life voters, I am sick and tired of Republican politicians that use the Pro-Life label to get our votes but then once they get into office they just keep voting in favor of funding for Planned Parenthood year after year. Planned Parenthood must be defunded as soon as possible, and it will be a great day in America when every Planned Parenthood clinic in the entire country is finally shut down for good.

2nd Amendment: I steadfastly oppose any efforts to restrict the freedoms guaranteed to the American people by the 2nd Amendment of the Constitution. Gun-related crime is the worst in cities such as Chicago that have implemented extremely strict gun control measures. When criminals know that average citizens may be armed, they are less likely to break into homes. Here in north Idaho, any criminal that intended to make a living breaking into homes would have a very short career indeed. No politician in America is going to be more pro-gun than me, and I am very proud to stand with those that work tirelessly to protest our 2nd Amendment rights.

Globalism: President Trump's "America First" message greatly resonated with conservative voters all over the country during the 2016 election. I am proud to stand with President Trump, and we must greatly resist the efforts of the globalists to slowly but surely erode our national sovereignty through a series of interlocking international treaties and agreements. Instead of merging America into a "global system", we need to focus on "making America great again".

The Federal Reserve: The Fed is at the very heart of our debt-based financial system. Since it was created in 1913, the value of the U.S. dollar has fallen by about 98 percent and the U.S. national debt has gotten more than 5000 times larger. The Federal Reserve was designed to create a debt spiral from which our government would never be able to escape, and that is precisely what has happened. Eliminating the Federal Reserve and breaking free of this debt-based system is one of the keys to a bright economic future for America.

National Debt: Barack Obama and his friends in Congress added 9.3 trillion dollars to the U.S. national debt over eight years, and so now we are nearly 20 trillion dollars in debt. Thomas Jefferson was correct when he said that government debt was a way for one generation to steal money from another generation, and at this point we are stealing more than 100 million dollars from future generations of Americans every single hour of every single day. This is a major national crisis that must be addressed immediately.

The Economy: I have spent many years documenting America's economic problems. Barack Obama was the only president in U.S. history to never have a single year when the U.S. economy grew by at least 3 percent, and economic growth has slowed down even more so far in 2017. If we want the U.S. economy to be great again, we desperately need to start returning to free market principles.

Reducing Taxes: Lowering tax rates is not nearly enough. Eventually, I would like to completely abolish the individual income tax and shut down the Internal Revenue Service. The greatest era of economic growth in all of U.S. history was when there was no individual income tax, and I believe that we can eventually return to those days. In the short-term, I will work with other Republicans to lower tax rates as much as possible, especially on the middle class, entrepreneurs and small businesses. And those tax cuts would be paid for by reducing the size and scale of the federal government to more appropriate levels.

Social Security: Tens of millions of Americans rely on Social Security today, and tens of millions more are counting on it being there as they rapidly approach their retirement years. Unfortunately, due to decades of bad decisions the future of Social Security looks bleak right now, and it is imperative that we strengthen the program so that it will be there for all of us in the future. I also believe that we should stop taxing Social Security benefits immediately.

Trade: Over the past several decades, the United States has seen tens of thousands of manufacturing facilities shut down. We have lost millions of good paying jobs and billions of dollars of tax revenue. We will always need to trade with other nations, but we cannot afford to keep running such huge trade deficits. I agree with President Trump that our current trade deals are very bad deals for America, and we need to replace them with balanced deals that will bring factories and jobs back to the United States.

Education: I strongly believe in parental choice when it comes to education. Our system of public education is a giant mess, and so many parents have turned to homeschooling and private schools as alternatives. I would abolish Common Core and the U.S. Department of Education, and I would return full control over education to the state level.

Hardening The Electrical Grid: A massive electromagnetic pulse that could take down our national power grid for an extended period of time could be produced by a nuclear weapon, but it could also be produced by solar activity. We have had several near misses in recent years, and scientists assure us that it is only a matter of time before another "Carrington Event" happens. It is absolutely imperative that we spend the few billion dollars that it would take to protect our electrical grid against such a disaster.

Homeland Security: I have great respect for those that work very hard to protect us every day, but without a doubt there have been many instances of abuse over the years. It is imperative that our security officials protect the rights and dignity of ordinary Americans at the same time that they are protecting us from terror.

The Surveillance Society: I believe that it is unconstitutional for the federal government to be monitoring our communications. I will push to have these unconstitutional programs shut down as quickly as possible.

Foreign Policy: I believe that the United States should have the most powerful military in the entire world, but that we should also be very hesitant to become entangled in foreign conflicts. I strongly support the fight against ISIS, but I very strongly believe that it is not in the interest of the United States to become involved in the civil war in Syria. Whenever possible we should pursue peace with our neighbors around the world, and having a strong, prepared and vibrant military is one of the keys to achieving a long and lasting peace.

Islamic Terrorism: In this politically-correct era, many politicians won't even say the phrase "Islamic terrorism" anymore. That is definitely not the case with me. The number of Islamic terror attacks just keeps rising with each passing year, and the western world must strongly confront this rising threat.

Israel: The Bible says that those that bless Israel will be blessed and those that curse Israel will be cursed. I will always stand with Israel, and if I am elected the Jewish people will have no greater ally in the United States Congress than me. I am 100 percent against a "two state solution", and I would use the full power of my office to fight against the establishment of a Palestinian state.

Race Relations: The Declaration of Independence says that "all men are created equal, that they are endowed by their Creator with certain unalienable Rights, that among these are Life, Liberty and the pursuit of Happiness." Instead of allowing the color of our skin to divide us, we need to start learning how to love one another deeply and with sincerity. Every precious life is of extraordinary value to God, and we should view each other the same way.

Abortion: Since Roe v. Wade was decided in 1973, nearly 60 million babies have been murdered in America. I am 100% Pro-Life, and I will work tirelessly to end abortion in America. I greatly applaud President Trump for nominating judges that are Pro-Life, and any Republican politician that currently holds office in the entire nation that is not Pro-Life should be immediately challenged for their position by someone that is Pro-Life.

Health Care: I am for a 100% repeal of Obamacare. But of course that won't fix our rapidly failing health care system. Ordinary families all over America are being financially crippled by rapidly rising health insurance premiums, and we need to rebuild the way that we approach health care from the ground up. I believe that a return to true competition and free market principles would do much to lower costs and restore sanity to the system.

Health Freedom: I am a very strong advocate for health freedom. I believe that the government should be encouraging natural health remedies instead of discouraging them, I believe that parents should always make the health decisions for their own children, and I believe that genetically-modified foods should be clearly labeled so that we can know what we are eating.

Immigration: America is a land of immigrants, but the way that we are approaching immigration today is entirely messed up. We make it exceedingly difficult to come in legally through the front door, but meanwhile we are leaving the back door completely wide open for criminals, gang members, drug dealers and those that want to abuse the system. So we are keeping out the hard working, law-abiding people that we should want to come to this country, and we are allowing in law breakers that are causing havoc in communities all over America. We need to ensure that everyone comes in through the front door, and that is why I support President Trump's call for a border wall and greatly increased security along our southern border.

The Environment: I believe that we all have a duty to help care for the environment, but I also believe that the way that the federal government is approaching these issues is completely wrong. The EPA has become a tool that the left has used to push a radical political agenda, and I believe that the agency should be completely abolished. In Idaho, the EPA has done much to harm the mining and logging industries, and I believe that it should be up to the people of Idaho to determine how the natural resources in our state should be managed.

Agenda 21/Agenda 2030: I am very strongly against the UN's Agenda 2030 and its predecessor Agenda 21. We should not allow the UN to be setting environmental policy, and I will firmly resist any attempts to implement any UN environmental program inside the United States.

Jobs: One of the biggest problems that Idaho residents have to face is a lack of good paying jobs. I will use the power of my office to promote economic growth and job creation in Idaho and for all Americans, and I believe that a return to free market principles will mean a more prosperous future for all of us.

Term Limits: America does not need a permanent ruling class of career politicians. My long-term goal would be to limit all members of the House and all members of the Senate to just one term, but initially it will be a really tough fight to get members of Congress to agree to any sort of limits on their political careers. But just because it will be tough does not mean that we shouldn't try.

Principles & Values: Jesus Christ is my Lord and Savior, and the principles and values that I base my decisions upon come from the Word of God. I am a family man, and I want my two-year-old daughter to be able to look forward to a bright future. But the only way that this nation is going to have a bright future is if we turn back to God. Our founders were men of faith, and they were not ashamed of this fact at all. In fact, the second president of the United States, John Adams, once made the following statement...

"The general principles on which the fathers achieved independence were the general principles of Christianity. I will avow that I then believed, and now believe, that those general principles of Christianity are as eternal and immutable as the existence and attributes of God."

If we truly want to make America great again, we need to return to the values and the principles that made America great in the first place. I know that many liberals believe that those values and principles should be completely discarded in our day and time, but that is something with which I completely disagree. We are in a battle for the soul of our nation, and it is a battle that we cannot afford to lose.

For much more information on my campaign, please visit MichaelSnyderForCongress.com.

-CHAPTER TWENTY SIX-

The Most Important Thing

Power to live a life that really matters only comes from one place. Perhaps you have been reading this book and you have been thinking that you are not sure if you belong to Jesus or not. The good news is that you can know for certain where you will spend eternity, and God wants you to be part of His family.

Yes, the years immediately ahead of us are going to be extremely challenging. And if you are a Christian, you will likely face persecution for what you believe.

But things are going to be even harder for those that do not know Jesus. Personally, I have no idea how anyone is going to make it through what is coming without a strong relationship with God. I know that I wouldn't want to face the years ahead without Him.

And it is a fact that this life does not go on indefinitely. There are some people that get insurance policies for just about anything and everything, but they don't even give a second thought to what will happen to them once they die.

At the end of every book that I write, I like to include a section on the most important thing that I could possibly talk about. If I had not given my life to the Lord Jesus Christ, I would probably be dead today. He has taken the broken pieces of my life and has turned them into a beautiful thing, and He can do the same thing for you.

If you would like to know how you can become a Christian, I encourage you to keep reading. A lot of the time people find Christianity to be very confusing. In the following pages, I have tried to explain the core of the Christian faith in a way that hopefully just about everyone will be able to understand.

Fortunately, the Christian gospel is very, very simple to understand, and the stakes are incredibly high.

If Christianity is true, then it is possible to have eternal life.

I am not just talking about living for millions of years or billions of years.

I am talking about living for eternity.

If you had the opportunity to live forever, would you take it?

Many people would respond by saying that they are not sure if living forever in a world like ours would be desirable, but what if you could live forever in a world where everything had been set right?

What if you could live forever in a perfect world where there is no more evil or suffering or pain?

Would you want that?

The truth is that this is exactly what God wants for you. He loves you very much and He wants to spend forever with you.

If you could, would you want to spend forever with Him?

If God is real, and there really is an afterlife, who wouldn't want to spend eternity with Him?

To be honest with you, if eternal life really exists, there is not a single issue of greater importance for every man, woman and child on the entire planet.

Who would not be willing to give up everything that they own to live forever in paradise surrounded by people that love them?

All over the world people perform all kinds of religious acts, desperately hoping that they will gain favor with God. Some religious nuts even blow themselves up during suicide attacks, hoping that their "sacrifices" will earn them favor with God. But are those really ways to get to heaven?

Of course not.

God did not make it complicated to reach out to Him. The truth is that the plan of salvation described in the Bible is very simple.

It starts with God.

The Bible tells us that God created humanity and that He loves us very much.

In fact, God loves you more than you could possibly ever imagine. The Scriptures go on and on about how great the love of God is and about how deeply He cares for each one of us individually.

But there is a huge problem.

The problem is that humanity is in deep rebellion against God.

Humanity has rejected God and is continually breaking His laws.

Most people like to think of themselves as "good" people, but the truth is that none of us is truly "good". Each one of us has broken God's laws over and over again, and we are lawbreakers and criminals in the sight of God.

Perhaps you think that you are a "good person" and that God should let you into heaven based on how good you are.

If that is what you believe, ask yourself this question...

Have you ever broken God's laws?

Posted below is a summary of the Ten Commandments. Are you guilty of violating His ways?...

#1) You shall have no other gods before Me. (There is only one true God – the Creator of all things. Have you ever served a different God? Have you ever expressed approval for a false religion just because you wanted to be polite? Have you ever participated in activities or ceremonies that honor other religions?)

#2) You shall not make any idols. You shall not bow down to them or serve them. (The Scriptures tell us that we are to love God with everything that we have inside of us. Even if you have never bowed down to an idol or a statue, you may have created a "god" in your own mind that you are more comfortable with. That is sin. In fact, we are not to have any "idols" in our lives that we love more than God.)

#3) You shall not take the name of the Lord your God in vain. (Have you ever used God's holy name as a profanity or as a curse word? Have you ever failed to give His holy name the honor that it deserves?)

#4) Remember the Sabbath Day, to keep it holy. (Is there anyone alive that has kept this commandment perfectly?)

#5) Honor your father and mother. (Have you ever been rebellious or disrespectful to your father or your mother even one time? If so, you have broken this commandment.)

#6) You shall not murder. (Even if you have never killed anyone, it is important to remember that Jesus considers hatred to be very similar to murder.)

#7) You shall not commit adultery. (Sexual promiscuity is absolutely rampant in our society today, but you don't even have to sleep with someone to break this commandment. In Matthew 5:27-28, Jesus said that "whosoever looketh on a woman to lust after her hath committed adultery with her already in his heart".)

#8) You shall not steal. (Have you ever stolen anything from someone else? It doesn't matter if it was valuable or not. If you stole something, you are a thief.)

#9) You shall not lie. (Have you ever told a lie? If so, you are guilty of breaking this commandment.)

#10) You shall not covet. (Have you ever jealously desired something that belongs to someone else? This sin is often the first step toward other sins.)

The first four commandments are about loving God. In the Scriptures, you are commanded to love God with all of your heart, all of your soul, all of your mind and all of your strength.

The final six commandments are about loving others. In the Scriptures, you are commanded to love others as you love yourself.

Have you always loved God and loved others like you should have?

Sadly, the truth is that we are all guilty of breaking God's laws.

In fact, if we took an honest look at how guilty we truly are we would be absolutely horrified.

Take a moment and imagine the following scenario...

One of the biggest television networks has decided to do a huge two hour prime time special all about your life. It is going to be heavily advertised, and tens of millions of people are going to watch it.

Doesn't that sound great?

But instead of a two hour documentary about how wonderful you are, the network has discovered all of the most evil and horrible things that you have ever thought, said or did and they are going to broadcast those things to tens of millions of people all over the world for two hours during prime time.

What would you do if that happened?

Sadly, the truth is that whoever that happened to would be utterly ashamed and would never want to be seen in public again.

Why?

Because we have all done, said and thought things that are unspeakably evil.

We are sinners in the eyes of God, just as the Scriptures tell us...

"For all have sinned, and come short of the glory of God" (Romans 3:23)

God created us to have fellowship with Him, but He also gave humanity the ability to choose. Unfortunately, humanity has chosen to be in deep rebellion against God and we have all repeatedly broken His laws. When we broke God's commandments, our fellowship with God was also broken. By breaking God's commandments, we decided that our will would be done instead of God's will. And if you look around the world today, you can see the results. Evil and suffering are everywhere. God hates all of this evil and suffering very much. In the Bible, our rebellion against God is called sin.

As a result of our sin, the Scriptures tell us that we are separated from God...

"The wages of sin is death" [spiritual separation from God] (Romans 6:23)

So what can be done about this separation from God?

Why doesn't God just forget about our sins?

Well, the truth is that God cannot just sweep our evil under the rug. If God did that, He would cease to be just.

For example, how would you feel about a judge that decided to issue a blanket pardon for Hitler and all of the other high level Nazis for the horrible things that they did?

Would that be a "good" judge? Of course not.

There is a penalty for evil, and because God is just, that penalty must be paid.

Fortunately, Jesus Christ paid the penalty for our sins by dying for us on the cross. He took the punishment that we deserved...

"But God commendeth his love toward us, in that, while we were yet sinners, Christ died for us." (Romans 5:8)

We were guilty, but the Son of God, Jesus Christ, died in our place.

Being fully man, Jesus could die for the sins of mankind.

Being fully God, Jesus could die for an infinite number of sins.

He was mocked, He was beaten, He was scourged ruthlessly and He was nailed to a wooden cross. He was totally innocent, but He was willing to suffer and die because He loved you that much.

Jesus paid the penalty for your sins and my sins so that fellowship with God could be restored.

Not only that, but Jesus proved that He is the Son of God by rising from the dead...

"Christ died for our sins...He was buried...He rose again the third day according to the Scriptures" (1 Corinthians 15:3-4)

You see, if there was any other way for us to be reconciled to God, Jesus would not have had to die on the cross. He could have just told us to follow one of the other ways to get to heaven. But there was no other way. The death of Jesus on the cross is the only payment for our sins and He is the only way that we are going to get to heaven. In the Scriptures, Jesus put it this way...

"I am the way, the truth, and the life: no man cometh unto the Father, but by me." (John 14:6)

But it is not enough just for you to intellectually know that Jesus is the Son of God and that He died on the cross for our sins.

The Scriptures tell us that we must individually commit our lives to Jesus Christ as Savior and Lord. When we give our lives to Jesus, He forgives our sins and He gives us eternal life...

"But as many as received him, to them gave he power to become the sons of God, even to them that believe on his name" (John 1:12)

"For God so loved the world, that he gave his only begotten Son, that whosoever believeth in him should not perish, but have everlasting life." (John 3:16)

"That if thou shalt confess with thy mouth the Lord Jesus, and shalt believe in thine heart that God hath raised him from the dead, thou shalt be saved." (Romans 10:9)

So exactly how does someone do this?

It is actually very simple.

The Scriptures tell us that it is through faith that we enter into a relationship with Jesus Christ...

"For by grace are ye saved through faith; and that not of yourselves: it is the gift of God: Not of works, lest any man should boast." (Ephesians 2:8,9)

If you are not a Christian yet, then Jesus is standing at the door of your heart and He is knocking. He is hoping that you will let Him come in. He loves you very much and He wants to have a relationship with you...

[Jesus speaking] "Behold, I stand at the door, and knock: if any man hear my voice, and open the door, I will come in to him" (Revelation 3:20)

Jesus asks that you give Him complete control of your life. That means renouncing all of the sin in your life and making Him your Savior and Lord. Just to know intellectually that Jesus died on the cross and that He rose from the dead is not enough to become a Christian. Having a wonderful emotional experience is not enough to become a Christian either. You become a Christian by faith. It is an act of your will.

Are you ready to make a commitment to Jesus Christ?

If you are ready to invite Jesus Christ into your life, it is very easy.

Just tell Him.

God is not really concerned if you say the right words. What He is concerned about is the attitude of your heart.

If you are ready to become a Christian, the following is a prayer that can help you express that desire to Him...

"Lord Jesus, I want to become a Christian. I know that I am a sinner, and I thank you for dying on the cross for my sins. I believe that you are the Son of God and that you rose from the dead. I repent of my sins and I open the door of my life and ask you to be my Savior and Lord. I commit my life to you. Thank you for forgiving all of my sins and giving me eternal life. Take control of my life and make me the kind of person that you want me to be. I will live my life for you. Amen."

If you are ready to enter into a personal relationship with Jesus Christ, then I invite you to pray this prayer right now. Jesus will come into your life, just as He has promised that He would.

If you just invited Jesus Christ to come into your life, you can have 100 percent certainty that you have become a Christian and that you will go to heaven when you die. In 1 John 5:11-13, the Scriptures tell us the following...

"And this is the record, that God hath given to us eternal life, and this life is in his Son. He that hath the Son hath life; and he that hath not the Son of God hath not life. These things have I written unto you that believe on the name of the Son of God; that ye may know that ye have eternal life".

Do you understand what that means?

It means that you can know that you have eternal life.

The Bible says that if you have invited Jesus Christ into your life, your sins are forgiven and you now have eternal life.

What could be better than that?

But your journey is not done.

In fact, it is just beginning.

The Christian life is not easy - especially if you try to go it alone.

There are four keys to spiritual growth for any Christian...

#1) The Bible - If you do not have a Bible you will need to get one and read it every day. It is God's instruction book for your life.

#2) Prayer – Prayer does not have to be complicated. The truth is that prayer is simply talking with God. God wants to hear from you every day, and He will fundamentally transform your life as you pray to Him with humility and sincerity.

#3) Fellowship - The Scriptures tell us that we all need each other. Find a fellowship of local Christians that believe the Bible and that sincerely love one another. They will help you grow.

#4) Witnessing - Tell others about the new life that you have found in Jesus Christ. Helping even one person find eternal life is of more value than anything else that you could ever accomplish in this world.

If you have invited Jesus Christ to come into your life, I would love to hear from you. You can write to me at the following email address...

TheEconomicCollapseBlog @ Hotmail.com

We are entering a period of time that the Bible refers to as the last days. It will be a period of great darkness and the world is going to become increasingly unstable. According to Jesus, there has never been a time like it before, and there will never be a time like it again. But in the middle of all of this, God is going to do great things. He is raising up a Remnant that will keep His commandments, that will boldly proclaim the gospel of salvation through faith in Jesus Christ, and that will see their message confirmed by the power of the Holy Spirit just like the very first believers in Jesus did. This is already happening all over the globe even though no organization is in charge of it. And we know for certain that this Remnant will exist in the last days because the Bible tells us that it will (Revelation 12:17; Revelation 14:12). God is starting to bring things full circle. The Remnant of the last days is going to do things the way that the Christians of the first century did things. Have you ever wondered why so many Christian churches today do not resemble what you see in the Bible? Well, the sad truth is that over the centuries churches got away from doing the things that the Scriptures tell us to do, but now God is restoring all things. Without God we can do nothing, but with God all things are possible.

Today, we have an even greater opportunity than the first century Christians did in some ways. During the first century, there were only about 200 million people on this planet. Today, there are more than 7 billion. That means that there are about 35 times as many people living on the planet today than there were back then.

The global population has experienced exponential growth over the past couple of centuries, and that means that we have the opportunity to impact more lives than anyone else ever has. I believe that the greatest move of God that the world has ever seen is coming, and I believe that millions upon millions of souls will be brought into the kingdom during the years ahead. I encourage you to be a part of what is happening.

As the global economy collapses and unprecedented troubles break out around the globe, people are going to be looking for answers. Hundreds of millions of people will have their lives totally turned upside down and will be consumed with despair. Instead of giving in to fear like everyone else will be, it will be a great opportunity for the people of God to rise up and take the message of life to a lost and dying world.

Yes, there will be great persecution. The world system absolutely hates the gospel, and the Bible tells us that eventually Christians will be hunted down and killed for what they believe.

But those that have read the end of the book know that we win in the end. The Bible tells us that Jesus is coming back, and He will reign forever and ever. God loves you very much and He wants to make your life a greater adventure than you ever imagined that it possibly could be. Yes, there will be hardships in this world, but if you are willing to pursue God with a passion and become totally sold out for Him, you can make an eternal difference in countless lives.

When you get a chance, go read the book of Acts. Do you want your own life to look like that?

It can.

In these last days, those that have a passion for God and a passion for reaching the lost are going to turn this world upside down with the gospel of Jesus Christ.

The Scriptures tell us that "there is joy in the presence of the angels of God over one sinner that repents." When even a single person makes a commitment to Jesus Christ, there is great celebration in heaven.

As millions upon millions of precious souls are brought into the kingdom in the years ahead, what do you think the atmosphere in heaven is going to look like?

Yes, darkness and evil will also prosper in the days ahead. A one world government, a one world economy and a one world religion are coming. This world system will utterly hate the Remnant and will try to crush us with everything that they have got.

It is going to take great strength and great courage to stand against the world system in the times that are coming. You have the opportunity to be a part of a greater adventure than anything that Hollywood ever dreamed up, and in the end it may cost you your life.

But in Revelation chapter 2, Jesus promises us that if we are "faithful unto death" that He will give us "a crown of life".

For those of us that have a relationship with Jesus, we know that we have the ultimate happy ending. Jesus has forgiven our sins and has given us eternal life, and nobody can ever take that away from us.

Life is like a coin – you can spend it any way that you want, but you can only spend it once.

Spend your life on something that really matters.

God is raising up a Remnant that is going to shake the world, and you do not want to miss out on the great move of God that is coming. It is going to be unlike anything that any of us have ever seen before.

If you enjoyed this book, I encourage you to also connect with me on the Internet. You can find my work at the following websites...

The Economic Collapse Blog:
http://theeconomiccollapseblog.com/

End Of The American Dream:
http://endoftheamericandream.com/

The Most Important News:
http://themostimportantnews.com/

Thank you for taking the time to read this book to the end. I would love to hear any feedback that you may have. Just like the rest of you, I am always learning.

My wife and I are praying for you, and for all of those that will end up reading this book.

May the Lord bless you and keep you.

May the Lord make His face shine upon you and be gracious to you.

May the Lord lift up His countenance upon you and give you His peace.

ABOUT THE AUTHOR

Michael Snyder is the author of four books, he has been a frequent guest on major radio and television shows all over the nation, and his websites have been viewed more than 100 million times. Michael's articles are also republished on dozens of other major websites, and this includes some of the biggest alternative news websites on the entire planet. Michael and his wife Meranda are deeply concerned about the direction that this country is heading, and they are working very hard to bring renewal to America.